DOABLE RENEWABLES

16 ALTERNATIVE ENERGY PROJECTS FOR YOUNG SCIENTISTS

MIKE RIGSBY

CHICAGO
REVIEW
PRESS

Library of Congress Cataloging-in-Publication Data
Rigsby, Mike.
  Doable renewables : 16 alternative energy projects for young scientists /
Mike Rigsby.
    p. cm.
  ISBN 978-1-56976-343-8 (pbk.)
  1. Renewable energy sources—Experiments—Juvenile literature. I. Title.

TJ808.2.R54

2010
  621.042—dc22

2010019520

Cover design: Scott Rattray
Interior design: Scott Rattray
Photo credits: Mike Rigsby
Illlustrations: Scott Rattray

Published by Chicago Review Press, Incorporated
814 North Franklin Street
Chicago, Illinois 60610
ISBN 978-1-56976-343-8
Printed in the United States of America
5 4 3 2 1

FSC
Mixed Sources
Product group from well-managed
forests and other controlled sources

Cert no. SW-COC-002283
www.fsc.org
© 1996 Forest Stewardship Council

RAINFOREST ALLIANCE CERTIFIED

To the unknown kid who is going to change the world.

(Please let the author know when you have succeeded,
so that your name can be placed here.)

ACKNOWLEDGMENTS

I wish to thank my wife, Annelle Rigsby, for catering to my time and space needs in the writing process. Renee Zuckerbrot, my agent, has continued to support and believe in me. Jerome Pohlen, my editor, has assisted not only in the writing process but also in moving gadgets around at the Maker Faire.

At the Maker Faire, Marc de Vinck made me feel much more important than I really am. My daughter, Tia Rigsby, volunteered to help with drawings and photography. Ember and Forrest Tanksley would have volunteered to help, but their wedding got in the way.

At work, Fran Shahbazian and Lil Wagner politely listened to my daily progress reports. Rob Phelan, when he heard of my hurricane loss, loaned me his old college textbooks. Eyra Cash, another engineer, provided technical advice, such as, "You're not going to use math!" and "I'm an engineer and I don't understand that."

ACKNOWLEDGMENTS

CONTENTS

INTRODUCTION

Years ago, Bishop Milton Wright brought a rubber band–powered helicopter to his sons, Orville and Wilbur, who were then 7 and 11 years old. The Wright brothers later claimed that their interest in flight began with this gift. Another child, age 5, was sick in bed. His father brought him a magnetic compass. The boy could not get the compass to point in any direction but north. There was "something behind things, something deeply hidden," he observed. The boy was Albert Einstein.

The world can be changed, turned upside down, by a kid with an idea. Perhaps even you. This book is full of ideas about renewable energy for you to explore.

Renewable Energy

As the world's population continues to grow, an increasing number of people will gain access to lighting, communication, transit, and computing. This increasing demand will strain the Earth's resources. We need renewable energy. If humans captured *one week's* worth of sunlight striking the Earth, the energy needs of the planet for *one year* could be met. Thomas Edison once said, "I'd put my money on the sun and solar energy. What a source of power! I hope we don't have to wait until oil and coal run out before we tackle that."

Wind blows your umbrella. Sun warms the Earth. Lightning strikes. The tide comes in. These forces all can be channeled into usable power. Renewable energy is the silent hand behind these events. Renewable energy is generated from sources found in nature, such as sunlight and wind. It is *renewable* because it is not used up and will be available in the future.

The plans in this book allow you to construct and explore working models that generate renewable energy. Most chapters include additional suggestions for creating science projects. The projects employ several methods for converting energy into useful forms. Remember, everything that moves, makes noise, warms up, cools down, or dries out requires the transfer of energy.

The plans in this book should be thought of as seeds—they will get you out of the ground, but they require innovation and work to grow into tall trees.

Most of these projects are, in a sense, solar powered. They convert heat into motion or heat into electricity. Because the cost of energy has been, in the past, relatively inexpensive, many of the devices around us have not been designed with much attention to efficiency. Wasted heat is common. Refrigerators cool your food but warm the kitchen, for example. This may be good in the winter, but in the summer your air conditioner must remove this extra heat from the house, which expends more energy and costs you money. You pay to heat the water in your shower, but also to warm your drainpipe—the water in the drain is almost as warm as the water coming from the showerhead, so most of the energy is sent down the drain. If you can find heat that is being "thrown away" and use it for a good purpose, you will be making the world a better place.

With today's technology, saving energy is more cost-effective than generating clean alternatives, so efficiency will be the focus of one chapter.

Thermodynamic limitations will be examined, too. For example, engineers will tell you, "You can't get something for nothing," and, "Low temperature heat engines are very inefficient." That being said, the energy that may be extracted overnight from 15,000 gallons of water—a swimming pool—can supply more electricity than is required to light a house for the entire evening.

Many of these projects are primarily for demonstrating certain principles, so they barely move, but others clearly have the potential to be scaled into real-world practice. Sunlight, concentrated on solar cells, produces electricity while also producing excess heat. Rather than being a wasted by-product, this heat can be piped off to a heat engine to increase the efficiency of the solar energy conversion.

The human-powered light system, aside from providing good exercise, can be useful in locations where there is no electricity. It also demonstrates the use of efficient lighting (LED lamps) and the future of electrical storage: ultracapacitors. Unlike batteries, ultracapacitors can withstand hundreds of thousands of charge/discharge cycles, so they rarely need replacement.

Safety First

If you work with energy, you need to be careful. Humans are delicate creatures and small amounts of energy can cause problems. To be injured by the sun, all you have to do is stand in it too long and you risk a nasty burn. And if you concentrate sunlight, it is easy to burn things, such as solar cells.

Melted plastic on my solar cell.

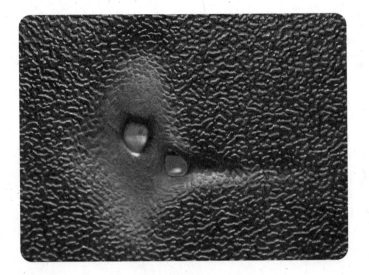

When you cut tin cans, you are left with sharp edges.

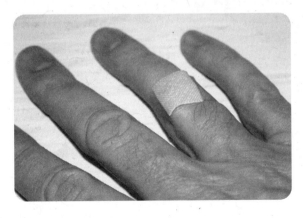

Based on my painful experience, do *not* place your hand inside a tin can for any reason.

Drilling, sawing, cutting, soldering, sanding, and painting all involve some risk. **ALWAYS WEAR PROTECTIVE GOGGLES.** Never look at concentrated sunlight. If you don't know how to safely do something, find knowledgeable help. Take your time and don't work when you are tired or stressed.

1

SIMPLE HEAT ENGINE

I n this chapter you learn to create a device that will turn heat into motion.

MATERIALS AND TOOLS

Corrugated cardboard, $1/8$ inch thick
Scissors
Glue
Sewing needle, $1\,5/8$ inches long
4 rubber bands, 7 inches long and $1/16$ inch wide
60-watt incandescent desk lamp (or heat source)
Aluminum foil (optional)

Build It

Cut one **Rotor** (1A), three **Base** pieces (1B), and four **Sides** (1C), two with holes and two without (refer to template). The cut pieces, along with the needle and rubber bands, should look like the photo here.

The needle should be 1⅝ inches long. If your needle is a different length, adjust the width of the base. The base should be ¼ inch shorter than the length of the needle. The rubber bands I used are 7 inches long (cut apart and measured without stretching) and ¹⁄₁₆ inch wide. You can experiment with this, but a band that is too strong or short may bend the needle. But if the band is too loose, it may not contract properly when heated.

Glue the three base pieces together in a stack.

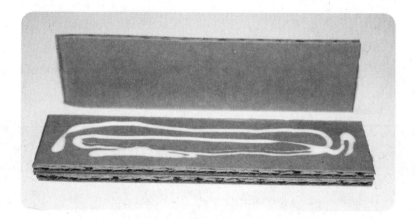

The complete base assembly should appear as shown here.

Glue the side pieces together in two pairs. Each pair should have one piece with a hole and one piece without a hole. Flip one of the assemblies around so that one hole is on the left side while the other assembly has the hole on the right side.

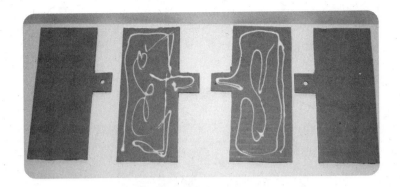

The completed side assemblies should appear as shown here.

Glue one side assembly to the base assembly as shown. Note that the hole faces up, toward the base piece.

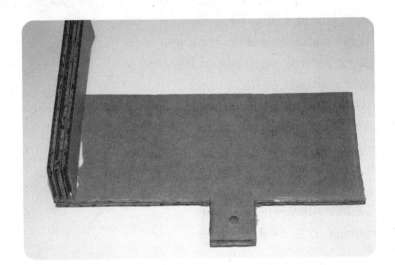

After the glue is dry from the previous step, glue the other side assembly to the base with the holes facing each other.

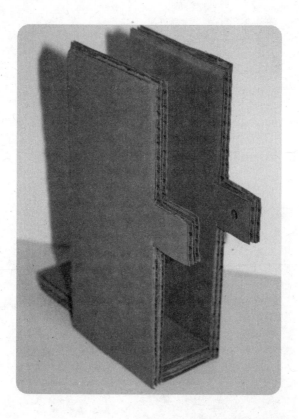

Now use the rubber bands to suspend the needle in the center of the rotor. One at a time, wrap the four rubber bands around the rotor and loop them over the needle as follows: place one end of a rubber band over an end of the needle, bring the rubber band around the rotor and loop the other end of the rubber band over the opposite end of the needle. Repeat this with the remaining three rubber bands, forming an X, as shown here.

Once the rubber bands are in place, the needle should be in the center of the rotor. Adjust the rubber bands to make them even by sliding them along the outside edge of the rotor. The tension on the rubber bands must be adjusted so that the needle is perpendicular to the rotor. Notice how the upper part of the needle is slanted (incorrectly) toward the left in this photo:

To correct this, pull the thumb (on the lower part of a rubber band) to the left while pushing the finger (on the upper portion of the rubber band) to the right. The goal is to get the needle—the axle on the motor—perpendicular to the rotor, as shown here.

Once the glue is dry on the base, gently pull the sides outward and slide the needle into the holes. The rotor should spin freely.

Place a heat source (a 60-watt desk lamp, for example) next to the rotor. Turn the lamp on and the wheel will rotate at a few revolutions per minute.

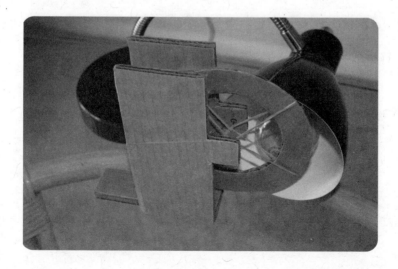

Do *not* use an open flame as your heat source. (Burning cardboard emits carbon dioxide—you don't want to spoil the atmosphere.) To keep the cardboard cool, particularly if you are going to run the Simple Heat Engine for a long time, you may want to attach aluminum foil to the outer side wall adjacent to the heat source.

How does this engine work? Most materials expand when heat is applied, but stretched rubber contracts (shrinks) as it warms.

With that in mind, consider the rotor at rest with no heat applied, as drawn below.

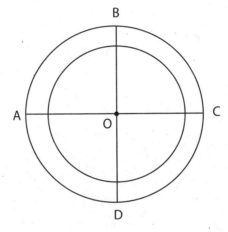

The rotor is balanced and is content to stay where it is. But when you add heat to the rubber band between A and O (which we'll call AO), rubber band AO shrinks.

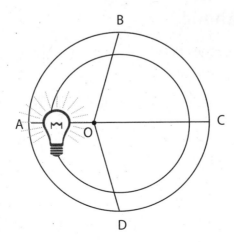

When rubber band AO is contracted, the rotor is unbalanced, which causes the right side to start rotating downward. Because there is more cardboard on the right side of O than the left, the right side is heavier. It will settle as shown here.

Now rubber band AO is away from the heat source, and as it cools it will stretch back to its original position.

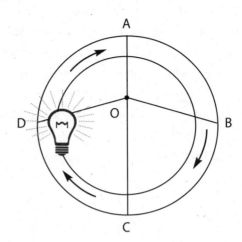

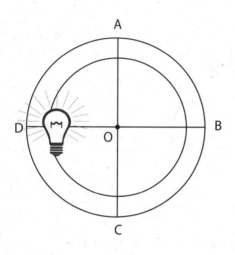

The rotor is now stable, but it has rotated ¼ turn clockwise. Rubber band DO is now in front of the heat source, and it will start to contract. This cycle will repeat, causing the rotor to continue its rotation.

This project works, but many questions are left unanswered. How long will the rubber bands last? How much stretch is optimum? What benefit can be obtained by adding more bands? How much heat can be added before problems occur? Where is the best place to add heat? Devise your own experiments to answer these questions.

More to Think About

- Will more rubber bands make the wheel turn faster?
- Will a larger wheel turn more smoothly?
- What happens if you use a heat lamp rather than an incandescent bulb?
- What happens if you use a fluorescent bulb instead of an incandescent bulb?

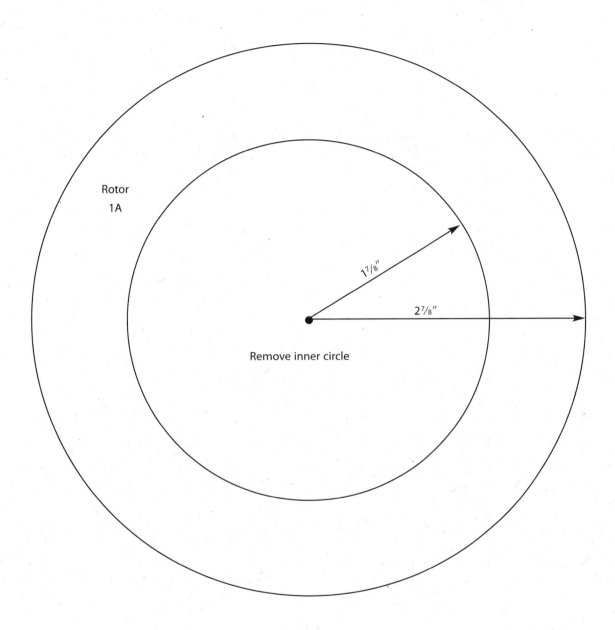

Rotor
1A

$1^7/_8''$

$2^7/_8''$

Remove inner circle

Base
(trace three)
1B

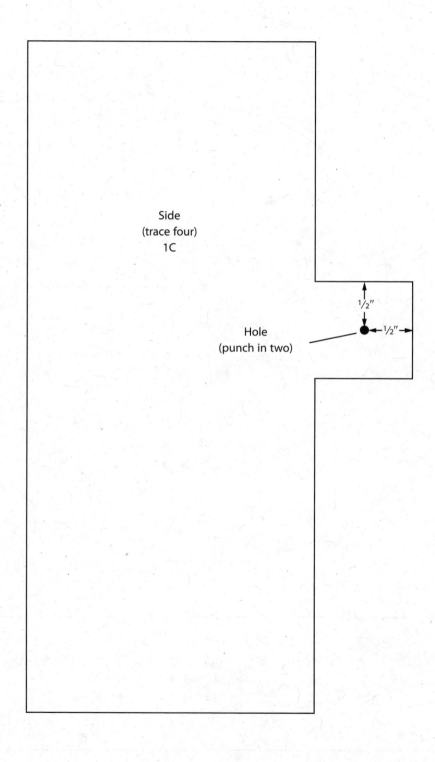

Side
(trace four)
1C

Hole
(punch in two)

$\frac{1}{2}''$

$\frac{1}{2}''$

2

NITINOL SPRING WHEEL

In this chapter you learn how to build a durable heat engine using nitinol springs. Nitinol can be costly—check your budget before you commit to this project.

MATERIALS AND TOOLS

Steel rod, $1/8$ inch diameter, $2\frac{1}{2}$ inches long
Steel ring, $3\frac{1}{2}$ inch diameter (craft store or old embroidery hoop)
4 nitinol springs (www.jameco.com, Part # 357835)
Magnet wire (#26), 10 inches long
Square aluminum tubing, $\frac{1}{4}$ inch square, 8 inches long
Drill
Wood base, $6 \times 3\frac{1}{2}$ inches, $\frac{1}{2}$ inch thick
Metal sheet, aluminum or stainless steel, 6×4 inches
2 wood screws
Heat lamp

Build It

Nitinol is a metal alloy composed of nickel and titanium. You can stretch or bend a nitinol spring until it appears to be damaged beyond repair.

However, when you apply heat (120°F or more), the spring returns to its original shape.

This Nitinol Spring Wheel will turn very slowly, about one revolution every two minutes. Yet because the springs can be stretched and compressed thousands of times, this machine is very reliable and could potentially operate for years without repair.

Start the construction by connecting the 2½ inch length of steel rod (⅛ inch diameter), the axle for the engine, to the 3½ inch diameter ring with one of the springs. I used part of an old holiday decoration for the ring, though an embroidery hoop will work just as well. Slip one end of the spring over the rod and the other end over the ring.

Repeat using three other nitinol springs until you have a spring-loaded wheel with the springs located evenly around the ring.

Using magnet wire, secure the four spring ends to the steel rod. I anchored this point about ¾ inch away from one end of the steel rod.

Next, make two supports for the steel rod. Using ¼ inch square aluminum tubing, cut two pieces, each 4 inches long. At a distance of ½ inch from one end of each tube, drill a ⁹⁄₆₄ inch hole through one side of the tube. *Do not drill through both sides of the tube*, since the back wall of the tube will hold the steel rod in alignment.

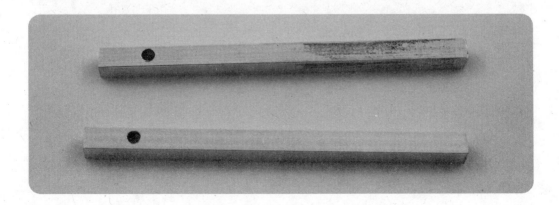

Use the **Base** template (2A) to cut a ½ inch thick wooden base, then drill two ⁵⁄₁₆ inch holes as indicated. Insert one of the tubes into one of the holes, as shown. The hole in the aluminum tube should be at the top facing in toward the base.

Place the axle from the ring/spring assembly into the ⁹⁄₆₄ inch hole in the aluminum tube. Fit the free end of the axle into the hole in the other piece of aluminum tubing as you push it into the other hole in the base.

Make a heat shield by fastening a stainless steel or aluminum sheet, 6 inches by 4 inches, onto the base using two wood screws, as shown.

Place a heat lamp near the engine.

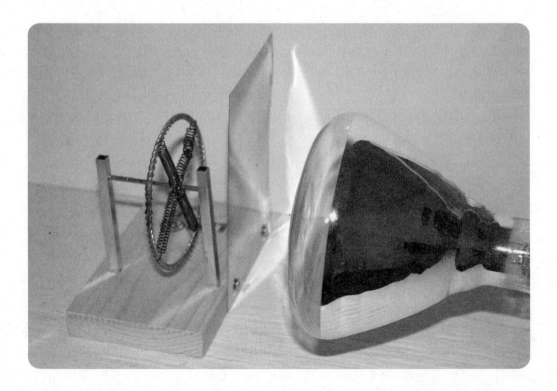

Viewed from the side of the heat lamp, the spring on the left will get warm and contract, much as the rubber bands in the previous project did. The contracting spring will stretch the spring opposite it (on the right), causing the wheel to become unbalanced. The wheel will rotate clockwise, bringing a new stretched spring into the heat where the cycle will be repeated.

In chapters 10 and 11, you will find two other versions of nitinol heat engines.

SPRINGS ON THINGS

Nitinol springs could be used to keep the sun out of a house by closing shutters when the sun reaches a position that warms the spring.

More to Think About

- Does the wheel move more smoothly with more springs?
- Does a larger wheel (stretching the springs more) help or hurt the engine's movement?
- Can you focus sunlight on a spring to make the wheel turn?
- What is the lowest temperature needed to achieve movement?

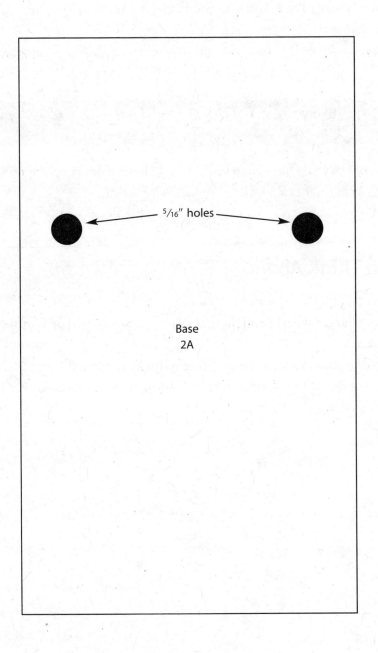

$^5/_{16}''$ holes

Base
2A

3

SOLAR DRINKING BIRD

The Solar Drinking Bird toy is a type of heat engine.

MATERIALS AND TOOLS

Drinking Bird (novelty shop or http://scientificsonline.com,
    Part # 3053617)
Black enamel paint (such as Krylon SCB-028 Flat Black) and paintbrush
Corrugated cardboard, $1/8$ inch thick
Scissors
Glue
Colored paint or crayons (optional)

Build It

To make the Drinking Bird drink, you usually place a cup of water in front of it. When you place the bird's beak into the water, its fuzzy head gets wet. Water on the wet head evaporates (unless the humidity is very high) as it bobs back and forth, cooling the head. The head, being cooler than the body, causes the liquid inside—a special liquid that boils at a low temperature—to rise up the neck, higher into the bird. The rising liquid causes the bird to become top-heavy and tip forward. When it tips forward, the head falls back into the glass and gets more water, while the liquid inside is allowed to return to the body. The cycle then repeats.

This is not perpetual motion or magic. The transfer of heat from the bird's warmer body to its cooler head creates the movement.

To create a Solar Drinking Bird, you also need to make its body warmer than the head. If you paint its lower body black and expose it to the sun, it will get warmer faster than its head. And if you shade the head to keep it cool, you will create the temperature difference needed to cause the bird to bob.

To start, pull the feather off the bird's tail.

Next, paint the lower body of the bird black.

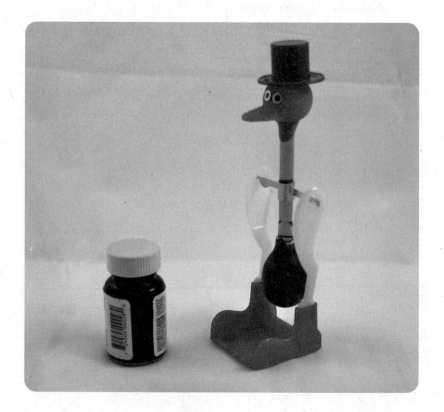

Cut a **Shade** (3A) out of cardboard.

Bend the shade on the dashed line, then cut out a 2 inch square cardboard **Support** (3B).

Glue the shade and the support together as shown.

After the glue is dry, place the shade assembly between the bird and the sun. The sun should shine on the bird's lower body, but not on its head. In a few moments, the Solar Drinking Bird should bob back and forth, and continue until the sun goes down.

You can paint and color the cardboard shade to make the project more attractive.

More to Think About

- Will a different color paint work better on the bird's body?
- Will a large hat on the bird work as well as the cardboard sun shade?
- Does the bird dip faster if the sun is brighter?
- Can you use a light to make the bird dip?

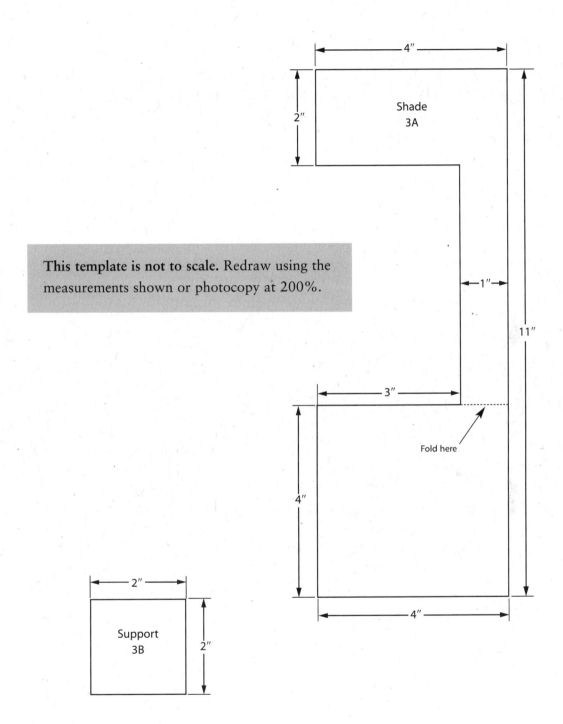

4″

Shade
3A

2″

This template is not to scale. Redraw using the
measurements shown or photocopy at 200%.

1″

11″

3″

Fold here

4″

4″

2″

Support
3B

2″

4

THE WAY THE WORLD WORKS

You can't get something for nothing. This is an important rule of physics, the main part of the Laws of Thermodynamics.

Yet it's tricky. Just because you "can't get something for nothing" doesn't mean you can't get something for *free*. On a chilly autumn day you can step into the sun and it will warm your body. You don't pay money for the sun, yet it will provide you with free energy.

To change heat into movement, as the Solar Drinking Bird or the Nitinol Spring Wheel do, there must be a temperature difference, a hot side and a cold side. If there is no temperature difference, there will be no movement.

Typically, when you take heat and change it into movement, most of the heat is wasted rather than being converted into motion. When an automobile burns gasoline, more than half of the energy is converted to heat. Only a small portion is actually used to make the car go. Unfortunately, the same is true of electric power plants. Usually more than half the energy goes toward creating heat, the rest being converted to electricity.

The amount of work you get out of a system compared to the amount of energy put in is called efficiency. The conversion of heat to motion is very poor, usually 15 to 30 percent, with 70 percent or more of the energy being thrown away as extra heat.

Why? There is another pesky "rule" from the Laws of Thermodynamics. Efficiency is related to the difference in temperature between the hot side and cold side of a heat engine. The hotter the hot side and the colder the cold side, the greater the efficiency. You can't get 100 percent efficiency because to do so a heat engine would have to lose *all* of it's heat. The temperature of the cold side would have to be about −460° Fahrenheit, the temperature at which there is no heat.

In 1824 Nicolas Carnot, a French physicist, described the Carnot cycle, which determines the maximum possible efficiency of a heat engine. Because real engines have friction and are made from imperfect, real materials, it is not possible to achieve Carnot efficiency. A precision Stirling heat engine (see Chapter 5: Stirling Engine) operating from the heat of your hand, is about one percent efficient—99 percent of the heat is thrown away. The same engine with sun shining on its black surface (about 150°F) is about 10 percent efficient (90 percent of the heat is thrown away).

The good news is that anywhere you can find a temperature difference, you can harness it to do work. The bad news is that the efficiency will be poor if the temperature difference is small.

Math Alert!

If you are curious as to exactly how the temperature differences between the hot and cold sides of a heat engine affect efficiency, a little math is needed. I will try to explain the Carnot efficiency formula as simply as possible.

To make the calculation, all temperatures need to be measured in degrees Kelvin. To change from degrees Fahrenheit (°F) to degrees Kelvin (°K), first convert degrees Fahrenheit to degrees Celsius (°C) using the following formula:

$$°C = (°F - 32) \times 5/9$$

Then change from degrees Celsius (°C) to Kelvin using the following formula:

$$°K = °C + 273.15$$

Efficiency (E), as a percentage, is determined by the following formula where T_{high} (in degrees Kelvin) is the hot side of your heat engine and T_{low} is the cool side of the heat engine.

$$E = ((T_{high} - T_{low})/T_{high}) \times 100$$

To get an idea of how efficient a Stirling engine would be in practice, plug in some numbers. What would a Stirling engine's maximum possible efficiency be when the temperature difference between the hot side and cold side is 7° Fahrenheit?

Assume the room temperature (on the cold side) is 72°F and the hot side (your hand temperature) is 79°F. First change 72°F into degrees Kelvin:

$$°C = (72 - 32) \times \frac{5}{9}$$

$$°C = 22.22$$

$$°K = °C + 273.15$$

$$°K = 22.22 + 273.15$$

$$°K = 295.37$$

Using the same method, change 79°F into degrees Kelvin:

$$°C = (79 - 32) \times \frac{5}{9}$$

$$°C = 26.11$$

$$°K = °C + 273.15$$

$$°K = 26.11 + 273.15$$

$$°K = 299.26$$

Now plug the high and low temperature values into the efficiency formula:

$$E = ((T_{high} - T_{low})/T_{high}) \times 100$$

$$E = ((299.26 - 295.37)/299.26) \times 100$$

$$E = 0.0129 \times 100$$

$$E = 1.29$$

The maximum efficiency of this engine is almost 1.5 percent. Over 98 percent of the heat energy cannot be converted into mechanical motion.

This formula tells us that the hotter the hot side and the colder the cold side, the better the potential efficiency in converting heat into movement.

5

STIRLING ENGINE

In 1816 the Reverend Dr. Robert Stirling invented a heat engine now known as the Stirling engine. Stirling was concerned by some of the dangerous steam engines of his time—they sometimes exploded and killed nearby workers. He designed a more efficient engine that saved some of the heat from one cycle and used it in the next. He called this feature an "economizer," though today it is called a "regenerator."

A Stirling engine can reach about 50 percent of the maximum possible efficiency (as defined by Carnot), making it one of the most efficient engines that can be constructed. The gas used inside a Stirling engine can be air, so no exotic materials are necessary for construction.

MATERIALS AND TOOLS

Stirling engine (www.stirlingengine.com, model MM-7)
Warm hand

Explore It

A Stirling engine can be built to operate on the heat from your hand. As little as a 7° Fahrenheit difference between the hot and cold sides of the engine is all that is necessary to make one operate. Today, most Stirling engines are built for educational purposes. The better the engine, the more it costs. Engines that will operate from the heat of your hand are skillfully machined (like a fine watch) and expensive (like a fine watch).

You can set one of these engines in the sunlight and it will work.

If you want to construct your own engine, go to a search site on the Internet and type in "tin can stirling." In a day or so, you can build a Stirling engine that will operate from the heat of a candle or focused sun rays.

If you put heat on one end of a Stirling engine and cold on the other, the shaft will turn. If you turn the shaft with a motor, one end of the Stirling engine will get hot and the other will get cold. Super refrigeration, down to about 10° Kelvin, can be accomplished by operating a Stirling engine in this manner.

With an engine that will turn on a 7°F temperature difference, many possibilities are opened. The heat stored in a swimming pool during sunlight hours could be extracted at night to turn a generator and light a house. Although the efficiency is very low at this small temperature difference, thousands of gallons of water store a significant amount of energy.

So why isn't this done? Mainly, the cost of building such a system isn't competitive with the low cost of electricity or other fossil fuel–burning sources. You do not need a college degree or expensive materials to build a Stirling engine, but the engine pictured above requires careful construction and precise components.

This is an old, proven technology. With the right combination of manufacturing technique and cost controls, Stirling engines have the potential to be widely used in modern society.

More to Think About

- When the engine just starts to turn, what is the temperature difference that you measure?
- If you apply heat to the top and cold to the bottom, what happens?
- If you set the engine on top of ice, will it run?
- If you set ice on top of the engine, will it run?

6

SOLAR SEESAW

I n this chapter you will learn to create a solar-powered seesaw. Sunlight, focused through a magnifying lens, will heat a bimetallic spring. The spring (taken from a large dial-type thermometer) will expand, changing the balance of the system. Unbalanced, the seesaw will move to the opposite position, moving the spring out of the path of the focused sun. The spring will cool and the seesaw will return to its original position to repeat the process.

MATERIALS AND TOOLS

Old CD
Scissors
Corrugated cardboard, $1/8$ inch thick
Hole punch
Epoxy glue
Pencil
Large dial thermometer with bimetallic
   spring (www.springfieldprecision.com,
   Model # 90309)

Aluminum rod, $1/16$ inch
   diameter, 8 inches long
Magnet wire (#26), or similar wire
Drill, $5/64$ bit
Aluminum foil
Wood blocks or books
Dark sunglasses
Magnifying hand lens

Build It

First, take a CD and cut it in half with scissors.

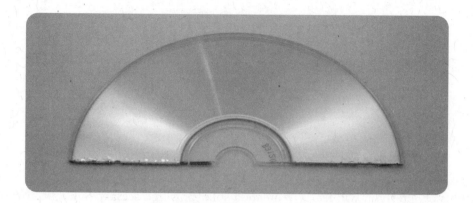

Next cut two **Beams** (6A) out of cardboard.

Epoxy glue the CD to one of the beams. It should be centered with the hole of the CD lining up with the hole in the beam.

Epoxy the other beam to the first beam, with the CD between them and the holes aligned, and insert a pencil (axle) through the center hole.

Obtain a large dial-type thermometer and remove the bimetallic spring. This will require removal of the clear plastic face. It can usually be pried off with a screwdriver. Next, remove the temperature dial—pull it or break it off.

Tie an 8 inch piece of $\frac{1}{16}$ inch diameter aluminum rod to the spring using magnet wire. I use #26 magnet wire, but any size should work.

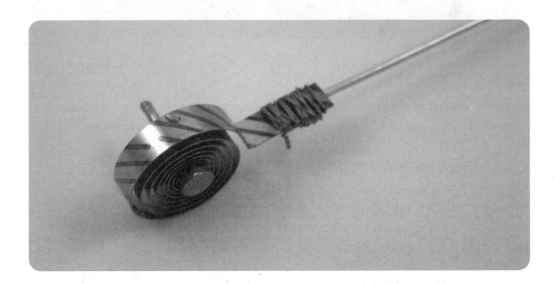

Find the top center of the CD (perpendicular to the beam, above the pencil). Drill a ⁵⁄₆₄ inch diameter hole in the CD near the top edge, as shown.

Insert the spring/rod assembly through the hole in the CD. *Before you apply the epoxy*, be sure that the spring/rod assembly will move to the left when heated. You can point a hair blow-dryer at the spring to test this. If the spring/rod assembly moves to the right when heated, then it must be angled to the left before glue is applied. With the rod at room temperature and angled to the right, glue the spring/rod assembly into place with epoxy glue.

Cut and prepare four **Supports** (6B). The holes in the support piece should be slightly larger than the pencil so that the pencil will move freely.

Align the holes on two support pieces and glue them together for each side support.

Cut out two **Base** pieces (6C) and glue them together to form the base.

Glue one of the support assemblies perpendicular to the base at the center. Insert the pencil/beam assembly through the hole in this support. Put the other end of the pencil through the second support assembly hole and glue that support to the base. Allow the glue to dry.

Take a small piece of aluminum foil and wrap a ball, about 1 inch in diameter, around the end of the aluminum rod. You may have to adjust the size of this foil ball—larger for a strong spring, smaller for a weak spring.

Place wood blocks, books, or cardboard under the ends of the beam. If the seesaw is allowed to move too far, the movement of the spring will not have enough power to move from one position to the other.

Put on a pair of dark sunglasses. Focus a magnifying hand lens on the spring. Don't make the focused beam smaller than the size of a small coin—you don't want to melt the CD. Even with the sunglasses, only look briefly at the focused spot. The spring should quickly move to the left.

Put down the hand lens. In a minute or so, the spring will cool and return to its original position. Pull out the magnifier and repeat the process.

More to Think About

- Is the cycle faster when you use a larger spring?
- Could you make this work by painting the spring black and shading the "cool off" area?
- If the rod is shorter, can you use the same weight ball?
- Can you make a seesaw that moves into and out of an air conditioner's cold air current?

This template is not to scale. Redraw using the measurements shown or photocopy at 125%.

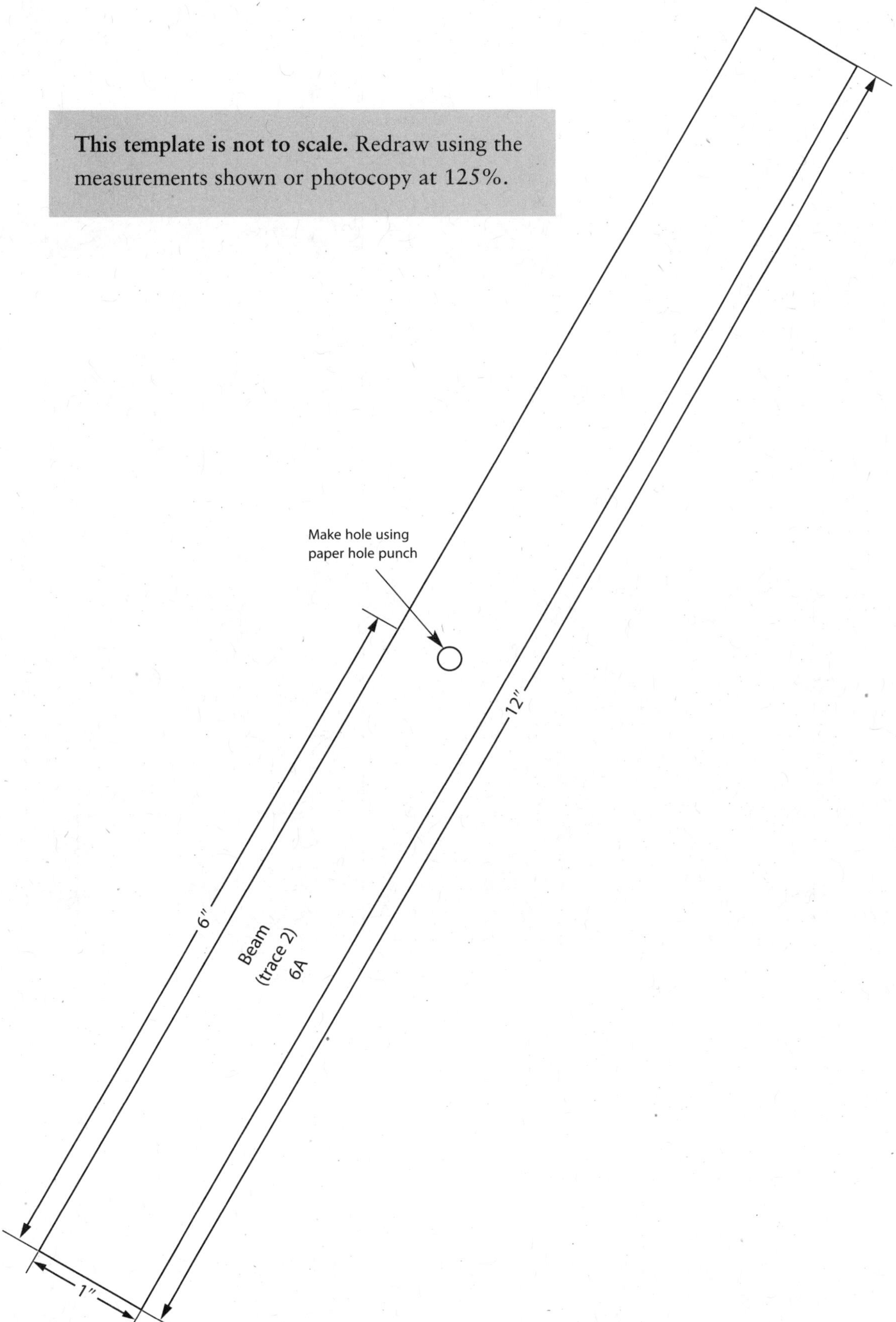

Make hole using
paper hole punch

12"

6"

Beam
(trace 2)
6A

1"

Base
(trace two)
6C

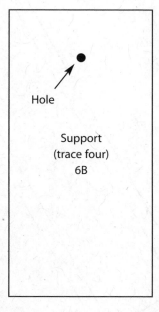

Hole

Support
(trace four)
6B

7

MEASURING TOOLS

Although it is fun to build things and just see if they work, the ability to measure temperature, power, and voltage are very important. For example, if you focus sunlight through a magnifying lens, things can get pretty hot. While you can watch for smoke or melting plastic, fires and burned fingers are not the best ways to monitor for excessive temperature. A point-and-shoot infrared thermometer enables you to determine temperature without touching anything.

MATERIALS AND TOOLS

Kintrex IRT0421 Infrared Thermometer (www.amazon.com, $47)
P3 International P4400 Kill a Watt Electricity Usage Monitor (www.amazon.com, $20)
PC Interface Digital Multimeter (www.jameco.com, Part # 117373, $79)

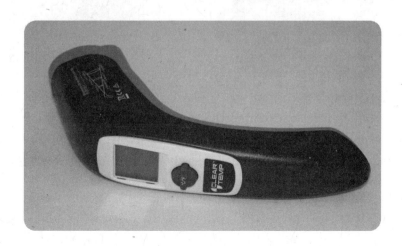

Explore It

If you point the Kintrex Infrared Thermometer at an object, a red laser dot indicates the center of the area where temperature is being measured. The temperature can be observed on the digital readout.

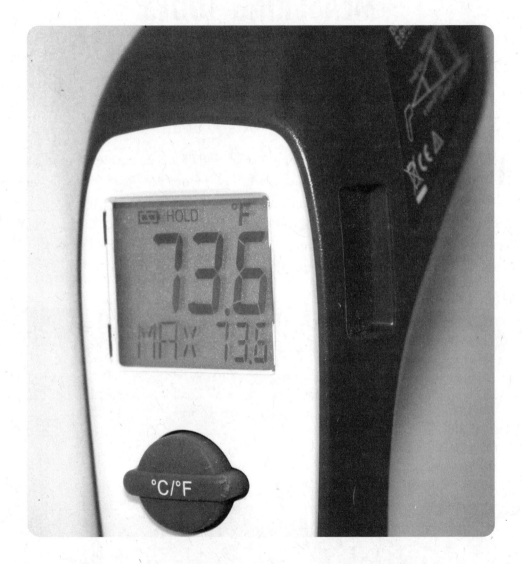

Because the reading is near instantaneous and nothing has to be attached, this tool greatly simplifies the gathering of temperature information.

To measure the efficiency of things that are plugged in, you need a wattmeter, in this case the P3 Electricity Usage Monitor.

By plugging a lamp into this meter and the meter into the wall, you can quickly tell how much power a bulb is using. This meter will log the power used by a device over time. Try plugging in a TV—leave the TV off—and measure how much energy it uses overnight. Many electronic devices still consume power while off. They are watching for remote control commands, maintaining memory, or they are just poorly designed.

Some of the projects in this book involve the generation of small amounts of electricity. To measure this power requires some type of meter. A digital meter is good. A digital meter that connects to a computer is even better, such as the PC Interface Digital Multimeter.

In electrical terms, power is measured in watts. Most digital meters do not measure watts directly. If you take a solar cell and connect it to something (such as a motor) then you may want to know how much energy the solar cell is providing under various circumstances. The diagram on the next page shows how to measure voltage and current with a

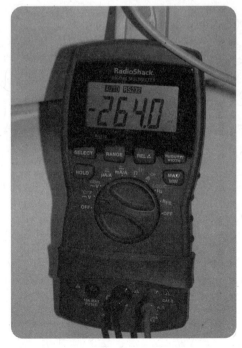

multimeter. To determine the power output of the solar cell into a motor, first measure the voltage across the motor terminals. Write this number down. Next, measure the current going into the motor.

Measure Voltage

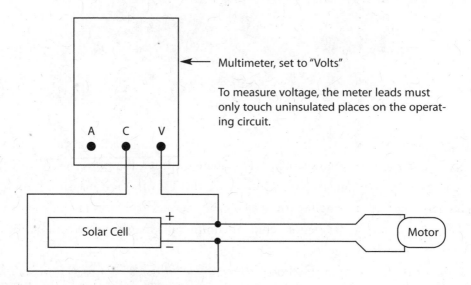

Multimeter, set to "Volts"

To measure voltage, the meter leads must only touch uninsulated places on the operating circuit.

Measure Current

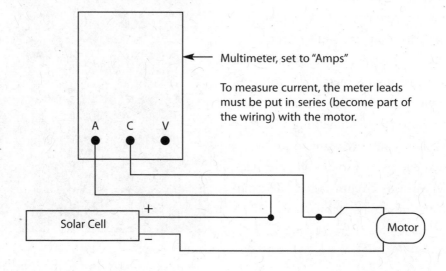

Multimeter, set to "Amps"

To measure current, the meter leads must be put in series (become part of the wiring) with the motor.

Power equals voltage multiplied by current. Multiply the voltage by the current and you will have the power output in watts.

If you are running an experiment, it is certainly possible to examine the meter every few minutes and write down the results. If your experiment runs all night, or during the day while you are away, this creates problems. If your digital meter attaches to a computer, the computer can grab your data—once per second, for example—and draw a graph for you.

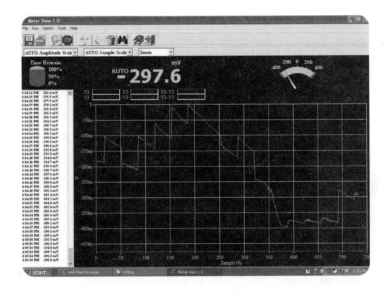

When working with small experimental devices, remember that small numerical changes can mean a lot. A voltage output of 4 volts instead of 3 volts is a 33 percent increase. That's big. If you tinker with a solar-powered engine and make it turn at 2 RPM instead of 1 RPM, that's a major advance.

8

SOLAR CELL WITH CONCENTRATED SUNLIGHT

In this project, you will attempt to increase a solar cell's output by concentrating sunlight on it.

MATERIALS AND TOOLS

Dark sunglasses
Solar Cell (Part of the Solar Project Fun Kit, www.radioshack.com, Part # 277-1201)
PC Interface Digital Multimeter (www.jameco.com, Part # 117373)
Kintrex IRT0421 Infrared Thermometer (www.amazon.com)
Flexible Neck Magnifier (www.electronix.com, Part # SD948)

Build It

Use dark sunglasses when working on the project, especially when concentrating sunlight with the lens.

First, use a multimeter to measure the output of the solar cell in bright sunlight.

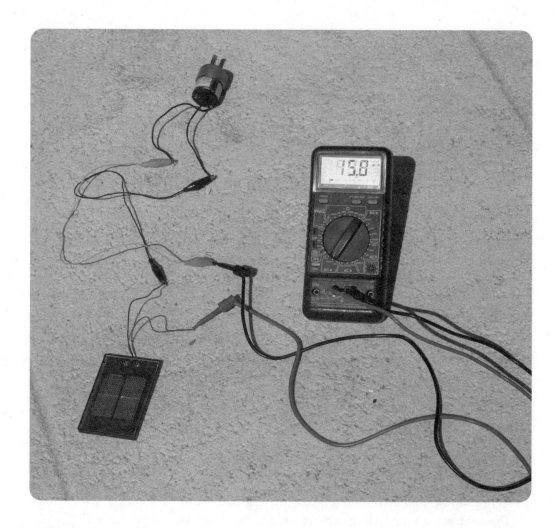

Measure both the voltage and the current. Multiply the voltage by the current to get the power output of the cell. Use an infrared thermometer to take a temperature reading of the cell. It is important to know how hot the cell gets under normal circumstances.

Now, using a magnifying lens, concentrate sunlight on the photocell. In this example, the actual photovoltaic cells (four of them) can be seen inside the module. It is not necessary to provide light to the entire module, only the area covered by photovoltaic cells.

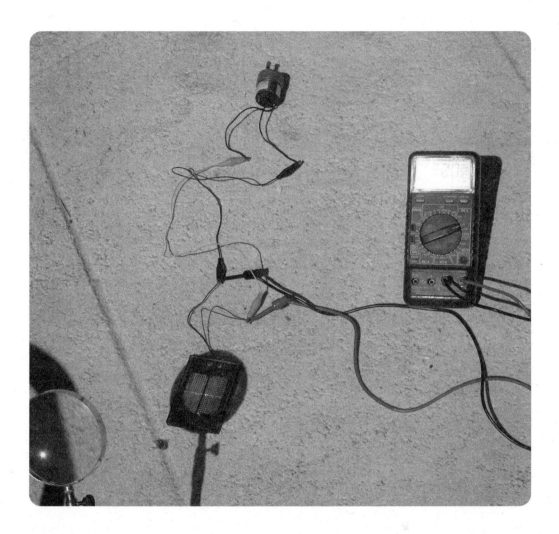

Again, measure the voltage and the current. Multiply them together to get the power output of the cell. The output should have increased by a measurable percentage. Check the temperature; the temperature of the cell should also have increased.

Increasing light on the solar cells through lenses or reflectors (such as mirrors) will increase the electrical output, possibly at a lower cost than purchasing additional cells. If the temperature gets too high, however, the cells could be permanently damaged.

Think about combining projects. More sunlight on the solar cells produces more electricity, but too much heat. Stirling engines need heat to operate. If you could pull heat away from the solar cells (a good thing) to operate a Stirling engine (another good thing), then you could increase the efficiency of the energy you have taken from the sun. If the leftover heat is stored in a tank of water, even more energy could be extracted at night.

More to Think About

- Can you increase the solar cell output by adding light with mirrors?
- Does this make the solar cell warmer?
- If you set the solar cell in a tray of ice cubes, can you add more light without causing damage?
- Can you use aluminum foil to increase the sunlight that strikes the solar cell?

9

WINDMILL

In this project, you will build a wind-powered generator.

MATERIALS AND TOOLS

8 wooden yardsticks
White glue
PVC plumbing connector, 1¼ inch inside diameter
Wind Turbine Generator motor (www.kidwind.org, Part # KWM001B)
Electrical tape
Drill
2 4-40 nut and bolt pairs, ³/₈ inch
Wood dowel rod, ⁵/₁₆ inch diameter, 10 inches long
Corrugated cardboard, ¹/₈ inch thick

Build It

Start by gluing three yardsticks together. Put glue along one end of one yardstick and glue it perpendicular to another at the 16½ inch mark. Do the same with the other yardstick three inches down at the 19½ inch mark. Glue another yardstick to the other end of the first three-yardstick combination, at the 16½ inch and 19½ inch marks, forming an I-shaped base. Because the glue joints are small, the white glue needs to dry for a full 12 hours before moving the assembly in any way that stresses the connections.

While that dries, glue two yardsticks together along their long edge, forming an L-shaped channel. Do this again with one more set of two yardsticks.

Glue the two yardstick channel pairs at the 18 inch mark of the base's two center yardsticks, as shown.

Now it's time to assemble your windmill's generator with the PVC plumbing connector and the small motor from Kid Wind.

Wrap electrical tape around the motor several times.

Push the motor into the PVC plumbing connector. If it is loose, add more tape. If it is too tight to go in, remove some tape, a little at a time, until the motor fits snugly.

Drill a ⅛ inch hole through a yardstick pair and through the back (the end without the motor) of the plumbing connector.

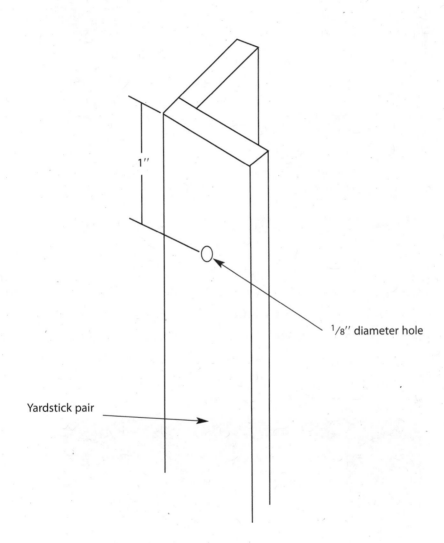

1″

¹/₈″ diameter hole

Yardstick pair

Fasten the plumbing connector to the drilled yardstick pair with a ⅜ inch, 4-40 nut and bolt.

Drill a ⅛ inch hole through the other side of the plumbing connector and yardstick set. Place the other 4-40 bolt inside the plumbing connector. With your finger inside the plumbing connector, pushing on the bolt, start to push the yardstick over the bolt. When the bolt starts to protrude through the yardstick, place the nut on the end of the bolt. Remove your finger. Tighten the nut on the outside of the yardstick set.

Drill a ⁵⁄₆₄ inch hole through a 10 inch dowel rod at the midpoint (five inches from either end).

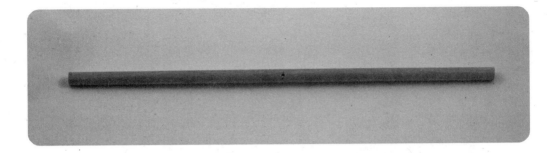

Cut two 7 inch by 2 inch cardboard rectangles. These will be the windmill's blades.

Glue the blades two inches from both ends of the dowel rod, one at each end. The blades should be oriented ninety degrees from one another. This means that when one blade is up and down (like a door in your house), the other blade should be sideways (like the top of your dining-room table).

Take the dowel and press it onto the motor shaft. This will take quite a bit of pressure as it is a tight fit.

The complete assembly should be fairly stable.

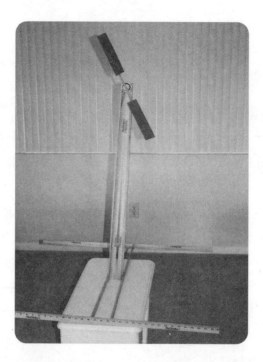

With a very slight breeze, the propeller will turn.

The electric motor, when its shaft is rotated, works as a generator. This is generally true for DC (direct current—meaning battery-powered) motors. This is not normally true for AC (alternating current) motors. For example, if you take an electric fan, unplugged, and rotate the blades, no voltage will appear at the plug.

You can attach a voltmeter to the motor (now generator) and see how much voltage it is producing in the wind. The voltage from the wind generator can be used to power a small motor or lights (if the wind is fast enough).

Changing the shape, size, and angle of the blades will change the effectiveness of the generator. Experiment!

More to Think About

- Do larger blades work better in low-speed winds?
- Does an angle different than 90 degrees work better to rotate the blades?
- Will four blades work better than two?
- How could you change this to catch wind that shifts directions?

10

NITINOL SPRING HEAT ENGINE

The Nitinol Spring Heat Engine is a commercially produced device that uses a long spring wrapped around pulleys.

MATERIALS AND TOOLS

Nitinol Spring Heat Engine (www.scientificsonline.com, Part # 3151809)
2 large plastic containers
Ice water
Hot water

Explore It

Place one side of the Nitinol Spring Heat Engine in a container filled with cold water—ice water works best—and the other side in a container of hot water. This heat engine has quite a bit of pull and it includes a gear that could be attached to a generator.

The spring transfers a lot of water between the sides and quickly evens out the temperature between hot and cold. Water is also sprayed for 10 to 15 inches when the engine is operating at higher speeds. Warning: the area around this engine will get wet. Don't place this on a surface that will be damaged by water, such as a fine dining table or your notes and books.

The nitinol spring contracts in hot water. This force stretches the part of the spring in the cold water so that it can contract on the hot side. Water collects in the coil of the spring, turning the engine spring into a virtual pipeline for transferring water between the sides. The transfer of water between the sides is a major obstacle to efficiency—the warm side cools and the cool side warms—but springs with a larger diameter might transfer less water. The transfer of water is not necessary for the engine to function, it is just something that happens because the design allows water to quickly move between the tanks.

More to Think About

- What is the minimum temperature difference to make this engine run?
- Can you reduce the splattering of water from the cold to the hot tank?
- Does this make the engine run longer?
- Can you make the engine run with room temperature water on the cold side?

11

THERMOBILE

The Thermobile is a clever device utilizing a loop of nitinol wire around two pulleys.

MATERIALS AND TOOLS

Thermobile (www.buythermobile.com)
Mug of hot water
Magnifying hand lens (optional)

Explore It

Dip, but don't immerse, the brass wheel on the bottom of the device into warm water (about 120° to 160° Fahrenheit). The brass transfers the heat to the wire, causing the wire to contract. This pulls the wire and starts the rotation of the wheel.

The big upper wheel (plastic) allows the wire to air cool and stretch. If the brass wheel gets too warm, the engine will stop turning. The wire must have enough time in the atmosphere to cool down, otherwise the wheels will stop. This device will rotate in either direction, depending on which way it is started.

It is not necessary to have water to operate this device. A small magnifying lens focusing sun on the brass wheel will also cause the wheels to turn.

More to Think About

- What is the lowest temperature at which you can make the engine operate?
- What is the highest temperature for operation?
- Can you place the brass wheel in ice water and make the engine operate?
- Will the air from a blow-dryer cause the engine to operate?

12

PELTIER CELL

The Peltier cell is a device that generates electric current when the junctions (sides) are kept at different temperatures. The cells are named after Jean Peltier, who discovered a cooling effect in 1834. If you apply DC (direct current) voltage to a cell, one side gets cool and the other side gets hot. This type of thermoelectric device was first discovered by Thomas Seebeck in 1821.

In this project, you will use the heat difference between two cups of water to operate a small electric motor.

MATERIALS AND TOOLS

Aluminum sheet (hardware store or www.onlinemetals.com,
  Part # 6061-T6, aluminum bare sheet 0.062 × 12 inches)
Hacksaw
Large binder clip, 2 inches
Peltier module (www.digikey.com, Part # 102-1678-nd)
Card, 1 × ¼ inch
Pencil
Pushpin
Motor (www.radioshack.com, Part # 273-106)
Tape
Cup of cold water
Cup of hot water
2 clip jumpers

Build It

First, use a hacksaw to cut two 4½ inch by 1 inch (¹⁄₁₆ inch thick) aluminum strips.

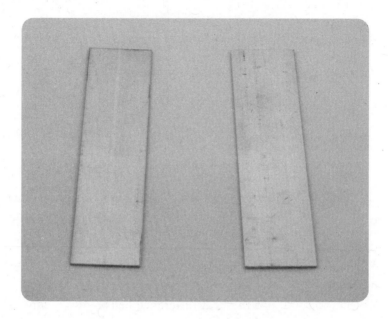

Next, bend the strips along their lengths according to the following drawing.

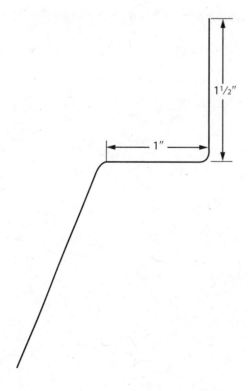

Place the Peltier cell between the two aluminum strips and fasten the assembly together with the binder clip as shown.

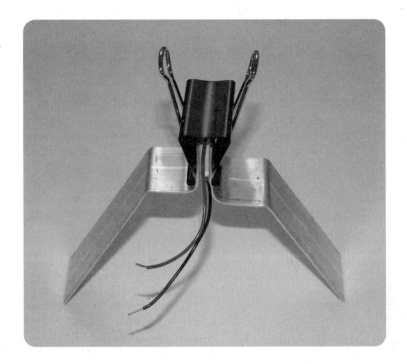

Cut a piece of stiff card—I used the edge of a business card—and shade the ends of the card with a pencil. The markings will make the piece more visible when it is spinning.

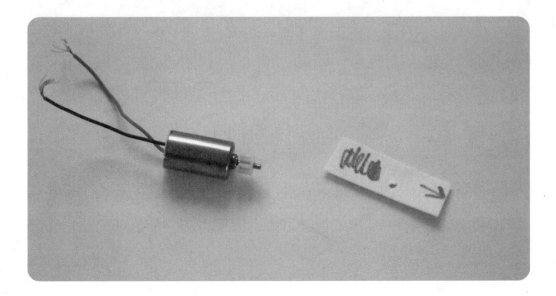

Using a pushpin, make a small hole in the center of the card.

Remove the vibration piece (the lopsided weight) from the end of the motor shaft. Push the card piece onto the end of the motor shaft.

Take a piece of tape and form a small roll, sticky side out. Place the tape roll on the top end of the binder clip on the opposite side from the wire leads.

Take the motor/card assembly and push it onto the tape roll. The card should extend past the end of the binder clip so it is able to turn freely.

Fill one cup with ice water. Fill another with hot water. Place the Peltier cell's attached aluminum strips into the cups. Attach a clip jumper to each wire coming from the Peltier cell.

Fasten the other ends of the clip jumpers to the motor leads. The motor should rotate.

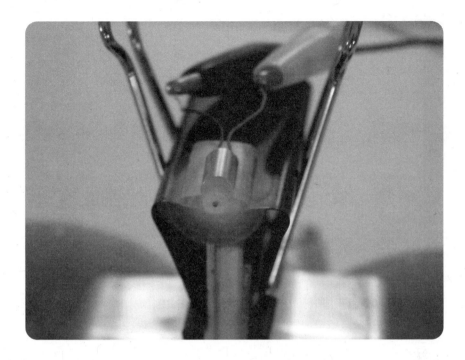

The assembly should continue to run until the difference in temperature between the hot and cold sides becomes too small.

More to Think About

- Why can't you make a large motor operate?
- Would the motor operate longer if you insulated the binder clip from the aluminum?
- What substance can you place on the Peltier cell to help transfer heat from the aluminum (thermal lubricant)?
- If the cups touch, what will that do to the operating time of the motor?

13

SOLAR CHIMNEY

A solar chimney is a device used to pull air (usually from a cool area) into a living space. Solar chimneys were used thousands of years ago by the Romans. Of course, they didn't have materials like clear acrylic, so we have more options today. Solar chimneys can be used as part of a passive cooling system, drawing air through a building without the use of a fan. Because hot air rises and leaves the room through a hole (chimney), a slight vacuum (shortage of air) is created. To replace the air that is lost through the chimney, air can be pulled from a hole in the ground (the temperature of the earth below ground is normally cooler than air on a hot day). The vacuum created by the rising hot air causes air to move without the use of a mechanical fan.

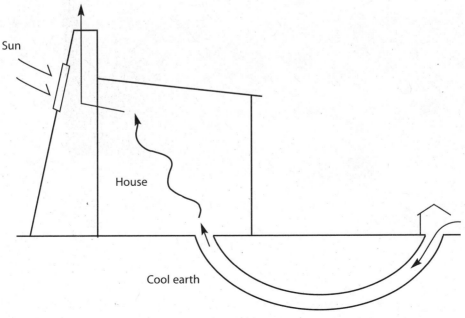

Sun

House

Cool earth

MATERIALS AND TOOLS

Wood, 2 pieces, 1½ × 1½ × 15 inches
Wood, 2 pieces, 1½ × 1½ × 24 inches
Wood, 2 pieces, 1 × 4 × 24 inches
Drill
Glue
2 aluminum sheets, 0.31 mm thick, 18 × 12 inches
Black paint
Plywood, 18 × 24 inches
16–20 wood screws
Silicon sealant (GE 100% Silicon Sealant comes in a "hand squeeze" tube)
Acrylic sheet, 18 × 24 inches
PVC pipe, ¾ inch diameter, 5 feet long
Electrical tape

Build It

You will build a device to demonstrate the possibility of moving air without the use of fans. First, drill four ⅜ inch diameter holes, three inches apart, in a 15 inch long piece of 1½ inch by 1½ inch wood.

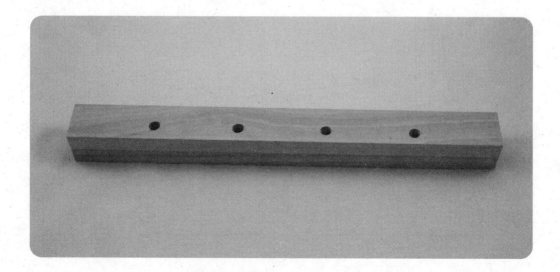

Cut an additional 15 inch long piece (1½ by 1½) as well as two 24 inch long pieces (also 1½ by 1½). Glue the four pieces together, creating a rectangle that is 18 inches by 24 inches, as shown.

Drill a 1⅛ inch diameter hole in the center of the top piece, on the opposite end from the piece with four holes.

Take two 18 inch by 12 inch aluminum sheets and paint one side black.

Place one piece of aluminum, black side down, on the wood frame.

Follow with the other piece of aluminum, also with the black side down.

Place an 18 inch by 24 inch piece of plywood on the aluminum sheets. Drill holes and screw the plywood through the aluminum into the wood frame.

Place silicon sealant on the inside edge of the aluminum and on the wood frame.

Drill holes through the acrylic, one at each corner and one in the center of each side. The holes should be larger in diameter than the shafts of the screws, but smaller than the heads of the screws. Place the 18 inch by 24 inch acrylic sheet on the sealant. Use screws to secure the acrylic to the wood—the sealant is primarily to prevent the escape of air.

Now make feet for the assembly so it stands on one end, with the four holes at the bottom. Take one 24 inch by 4 inch board and screw it perpendicular to the bottom of the frame, extending past the frame by one inch.

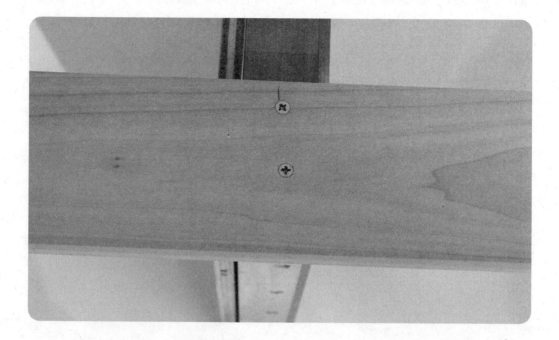

This board must extend beyond the frame so that it is off the ground, so air can enter the lower holes.

Secure the second 24 inch by 4 inch board on the opposite side of the frame.

Take a 5 foot long piece of ¾ inch PVC pipe and tape two rows of electrical tape around one end. This tape will be used to secure the fit when the pipe is placed in the frame.

Push the pipe into the 1⅛ inch hole in the top of the frame. If it is too large to fit, remove some of the tape. If it is loose, add more tape.

Place your chimney in the sun, with the black interior surface facing toward the sun. Hot air will soon rise out of the pipe. If you place smoke at the bottom, you should see it rise through the chimney.

Under the right conditions, the black aluminum plates will reach a temperature of more than 160°F. If the upper outlet were exhausted into a house (during the winter), it could be used as a source of solar heat. You can place a cooking thermometer in the upper outlet to measure the temperature of the escaping air.

More to Think About

- What happens if you don't paint the aluminum?
- If you don't seal the gaps around the acrylic, where does the hot air go?
- If you make two large holes at the top, what happens to the temperature of the output air?
- How would you change the design if you wanted to heat water?

14

RADIOMETER

The Radiometer is a device with four vanes, each with one black side and one white side. The vanes are mounted on a sharp point, for very low friction, in a glass that is sealed with some of the air removed.

MATERIALS AND TOOLS

Radiometer (http://scientificsonline.com, Part # 3060082)

Explore It

When a light (a lamp, a flashlight, or even a match) is placed near the Radiometer, the vanes will turn in a clockwise direction (as viewed from above). This assumes that the black vanes are on the left as you face the Radiometer.

The Radiometer will not work if the glass is filled with air and it will not work if there is a high vacuum. Although there is some debate over exactly how it works—a thermal effect at the vane edge seems to be the most credible explanation—the brighter the light, the faster the vanes will turn.

Try placing the Radiometer in a refrigerator.

Why someone first tried putting a Radiometer in the refrigerator is a mystery, but the experiment revealed something interesting: the vanes turn backward (counter-clockwise) while the device is cooling down.

More to Think About

- Will the heat from a hot stone (not glowing) cause the Radiometer to turn?
- Will ice cubes nearby cause it to turn?
- Why is this unlikely to be useful for converting energy?
- What is the smallest amount of light you can use to make the vanes turn?

15

KELVIN WATER DROP GENERATOR

In 1867 Lord Kelvin invented the Water Drop Generator. Falling water drops are used to generate voltage. Energy from the falling water causes the electrostatic charge on cans to separate, so positive and negative charges accumulate and grow on the connected cans. Because a naturally occurring, and very tiny, charge imbalance exists, the falling water drops enhance this imbalance and "collect" on the cans.

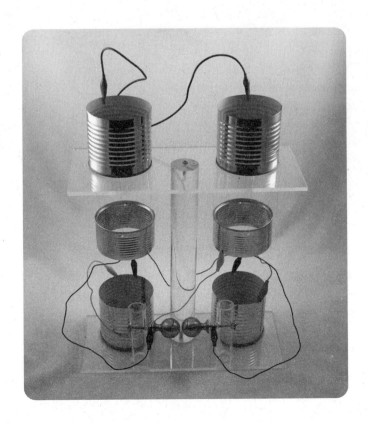

There is no way of knowing which side will be positive and which will be negative—it's random. The charge will cause a small spark to jump across the metallic spheres.

This device works best in a low humidity room. When the humidity is above 50 percent, you may have trouble generating a spark. Watch your weathercast.

MATERIALS AND TOOLS

Acrylic sheet, 12 × 12 inches, ¼ inch thick (www.estreetplastics.com, Part # 1002050100)
Acrylic rod, 1½ inch diameter, 12 inches long (www.estreetplastics.com, Part # 5007512100)
Drill
2 screws
2 acrylic tubes, 1 inch outer diameter, 4 inches long
2 round metal cabinet door pulls
Sandpaper
2 machine screws, 2 inches long, the same diameter and thread size as those that come with the cabinet pulls
Silicon sealant (GE 100% Silicon Sealant comes in a "hand squeeze" tube)
Can opener
2 cans, 2½ inches tall, open at top and bottom (8 ounce cans of pineapple are normally the correct height)
4 cans, 3 inches tall, open at top only
Fishing line, "20 pound test" or smaller
5 electrical clip jumpers
Water

Build It

Start your construction by cutting out and drilling the **Upper Plate** (15A) and **Lower Plate** (15B) from the acrylic sheet, as shown. Cut the acrylic rod to a 12 inch length and drill a small hole in each end.

Connect the rod to the lower plate with a screw. Note that the screw is countersunk—set in a hole so that the screw's head does not stick out and make a bump. To countersink a hole is to make it large enough to accept the head of a screw. In the lower plate, drill a hole that is larger than the head of the screw, but only drill about halfway through the lower plate.

Next, fasten the upper plate to the rod.

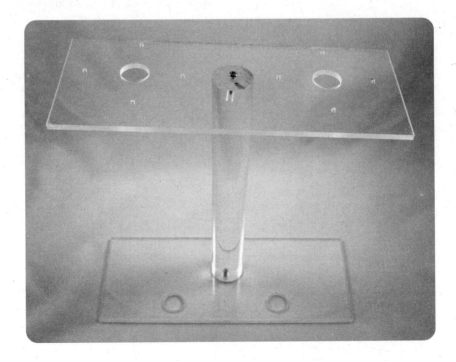

Cut two 1 inch diameter hollow acrylic tubes to 4 inch lengths.

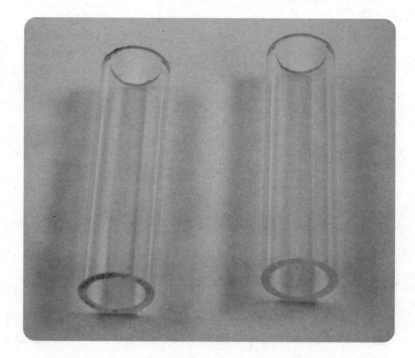

Take two cabinet door pulls (you want something perfectly round, but you may have to settle for something with a design) and sand them. Cabinet hardware makers normally coat the hardware to prevent corrosion. This coating inhibits our spark jump, so it must be removed.

Drill two ³⁄₁₆ inch diameter holes in each acrylic tube, 2½ inches from one end, and fasten the cabinet pull (sphere). Insert a machine screw in the acrylic tube and tighten the screw to the tube using a nut. The cabinet pull screws onto the end of the machine screw.

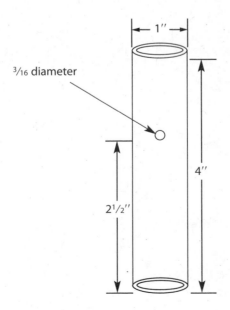

Glue the tube assemblies to the lower plate as shown on the template using silicon sealant. It will be necessary to support the assembly until the glue dries.

The spheres can now be adjusted (closer or more distant separation) by rotating them on the bolt assembly. The spheres should be approximately 1/16 inch apart.

Drill four 1/8 inch diameter holes around the 1 inch diameter holes on the top plate. They should be evenly spaced 90 degrees apart—one at the twelve o'clock position, one at three o'clock, one at six o'clock, and one at nine o'clock.

Gather your six recycled (empty) cans. Be very cautious when working with them since the edges can be very sharp. All of the tops should already be removed. Use a can opener to remove the bottoms from the 2½ inch tall cans. These 2½ inch cans will be placed in the center of the generator, suspended by fishing line. Drill four ⅛ inch diameter holes about ¼ inch from the top, each one evenly spaced from the next. They should match the spacing of the holes in the upper acrylic plate.

Using a 28 inch piece of fishing line, take one end of the line through a hole in a 2½ inch tall can and tie it to the line. Take the other end of the fishing line and bring it through one of the small holes in the upper acrylic plate. With the fishing line on top of the plate, take the line (90 degrees, clockwise) to the next small hole and insert it down through the acrylic. Push the line through the next hole in the can, then bring it back up through the upper plate, through the same hole where the line went down. Repeat this operation for the third hole. And on the fourth hole, insert the fishing line through the acrylic toward the can. Run the line through the fourth hole in the can and tie a knot. You should be able to adjust the can and fishing line so that the can hangs evenly about 3 inches below the plate.

Repeat this procedure on the other side of the plate. Both cans should hang at about the same height.

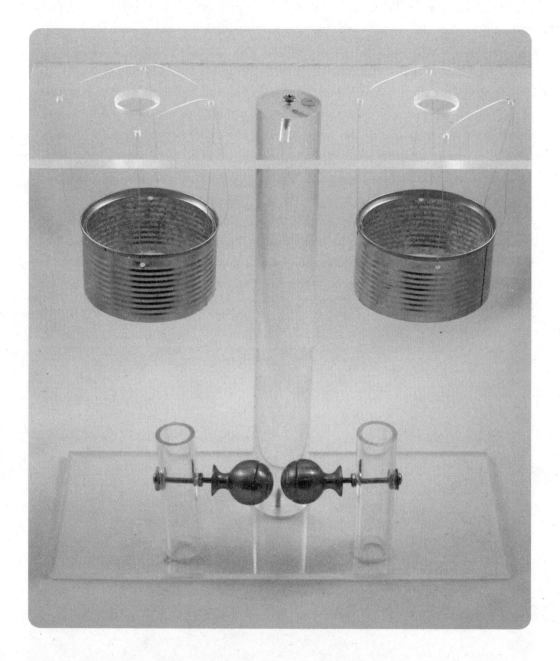

Drill one $\frac{1}{16}$ inch diameter hole in the center of the bottom of two 3 inch tall cans. These will be the cans that sit on the top of the generator.

Place the two remaining 3 inch cans (the cans *without* the holes) under the hanging cans. With an electrical clip jumper, connect the *left* hanging can with the lower *right* can.

Now connect the *right* hanging can to the lower *left* can using another electrical jumper.

Connect the lower *left* can to the lower *left* spark sphere.

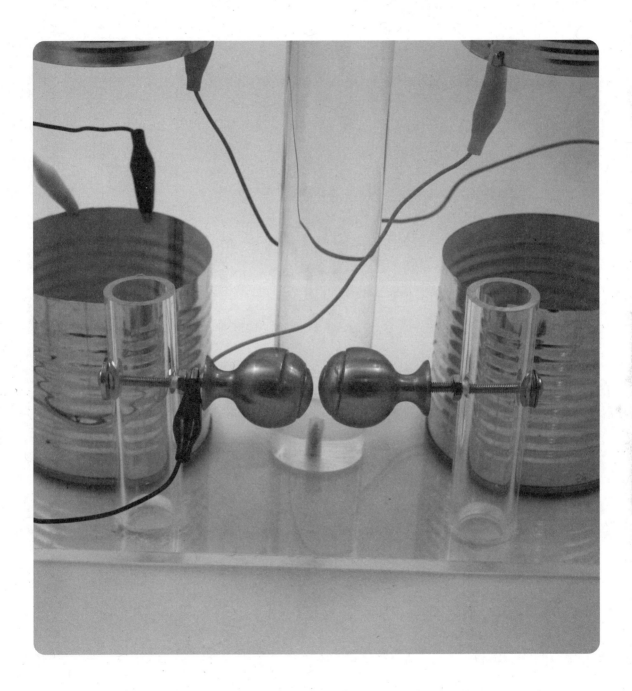

Connect the lower *right* can to the lower *right* spark sphere.

Place the two cans (with holes) on the upper acrylic plate. The tiny drilled hole should be centered over the opening in the upper plate.

Using a jumper, connect the two upper cans together.

Now the completed apparatus should be ready for operation.

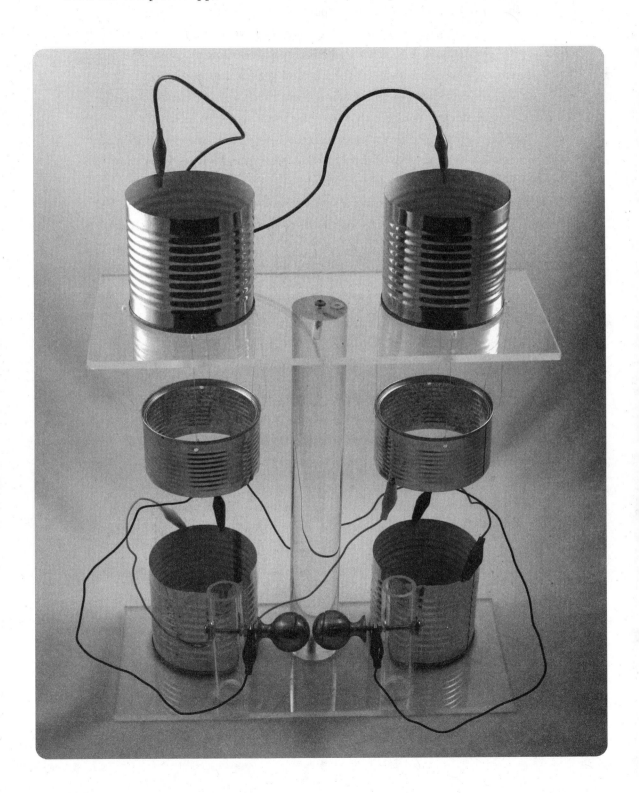

With the spark spheres very close (but not touching) add water to the two upper cans. If the humidity is low, and the apparatus is clean and dry, sparks should jump across the spheres. *Don't touch the spheres* or you will get a static shock (like scuffing your feet on a carpet and touching a doorknob). When the upper cans are empty, you can adjust the spheres and try for a larger spark.

You will have to disconnect the wires from the lower cans and empty the cans into a receptacle. (You're only removing these wires because they are in the way.) You can't empty the lower cans into the upper cans since the upper cans will immediately start to drip and there is no place for the water to go until you get the lower cans back in place and wired.

If you're having trouble getting a spark, check that the humidity isn't too high or that the spark gap isn't too wide. Both factors can prevent satisfactory operation.

More to Think About

- How do dirt and moisture affect operation?
- Will two small holes in the upper can work better than one?
- Does distilled water work better than tap water?
- Can you use a radio to detect "static" even when you can't see a spark?

TURN IT ON ITS SIDE

In concept, you could turn this device sideways and let wind push water droplets between screens to generate electricity. This would allow wind, rather than gravity, to be the source of power generation. Although a couple of older patents have been granted on this sort of wind generator, it is doubtful that an actual working device has been constructed.

If you were to compare this device to a windmill, what would be different? Would it be more or less efficient than a windmill? Would it be less of a problem for birds? What do you think this "sideways" water drop generator would look like?

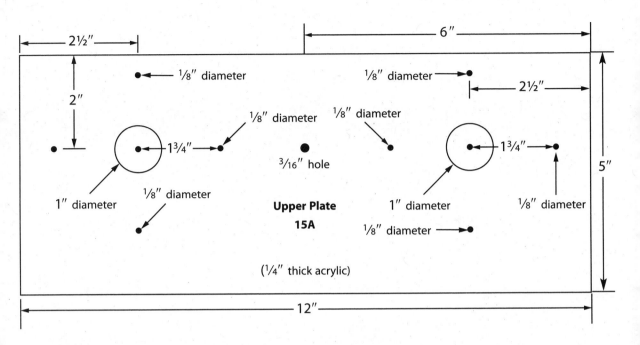

2½″

6″

⅛″ diameter

⅛″ diameter

2½″

2″

⅛″ diameter

⅛″ diameter

⅛″ diameter

1¾″

5″

3/16″ hole

⅛″ diameter

1¾″

1″ diameter

⅛″ diameter

**Upper Plate
15A**

1″ diameter

⅛″ diameter

⅛″ diameter

(¼″ thick acrylic)

12″

This template is not to scale. Redraw using the measurements shown or photocopy at 200%.

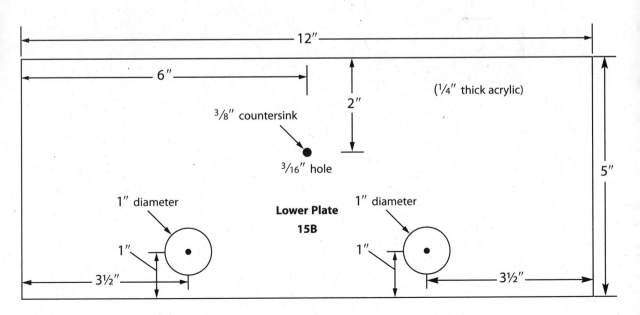

12″

6″

2″

3/8″ countersink

(¼″ thick acrylic)

3/16″ hole

1″ diameter

1″ diameter

**Lower Plate
15B**

1″

1″

3½″

3½″

5″

16

ULTRACAPACITOR SOLAR STORAGE

The sun doesn't always shine and wind doesn't always blow. In this chapter, you will examine a nontraditional way for storing energy and retrieving it as electricity.

MATERIALS AND TOOLS

Ultracapacitor (www.digikey.com, Part # 493-3317-nd)
Solar-powered light, single-battery (www.amazon.com, Mr. Light Solar-Powered Hummingbird)
Drill
Solder
Soldering gun
#22 gauge stranded red wire, 9 inches long (www.radioshack.com, Part #278-1224)
#22 gauge stranded black wire, 9 inches long (on same spool as red wire, above)

Build It

First you will take a solar-powered light and store the sun's energy in an ultra-capacitor. Ultracapacitors store and release an electrical charge. The process is kind of like scuffing your feet on a carpet—you build up an electrical charge that can be released by touching a doorknob. You are not chemically changed.

Because ultracapacitors do not go through a chemical transformation as they charge and discharge, they can withstand hundreds of thousands of charge/discharge cycles without damage. They can be totally discharged or very rapidly charged (think seconds or minutes instead of hours) without damage. Compared to batteries, ultracapacitors are larger and more costly. To release the electrical charge from an ultracapacitor, you must have circuitry that batteries do not require.

Choose a solar-powered light that has only one battery—fortunately, this is usually the least expensive type available. Open the light and remove the battery.

Find the wires that connect to the battery.

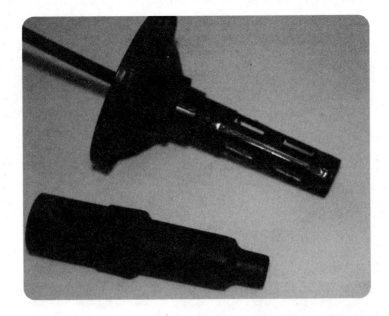

Drill a hole in the battery cover. It should be large enough for two wires to pass through, from the light to the ultracapacitor.

Solder a 9 inch long piece of wire to the positive terminal on the ultracapacitor. I recommend using red wire—red is commonly used for positive in battery-operated systems.

Solder a 9 inch long black wire to the negative terminal on the ultracapacitor.

Thread the wires from the ultracapacitor through the hole in the battery cover.

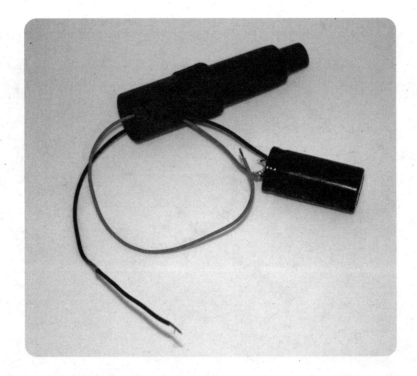

Solder the red wire to the light's positive terminal (the place where the battery's positive end was connected). Solder the black wire to the light's negative terminal.

Expose the assembly to the sun for a few hours, then take it to a dark place and you will have light without batteries.

More to Think About

- What happens if you add another capacitor in parallel (plus terminal to plus terminal, minus terminal to minus terminal)?
- What happens to the capacitor if you use a "two battery" solar light?

17

HEAT-POWERED FAN

Another method of storing energy involves heating water, then capturing the energy from the warm water and converting that heat to electricity.

Build It

Stove fans using Peltier cells can be purchased online, but they aren't cheap. These fans are designed to sit on the top of a hot stove and blow air throughout the room. Heat from the stove causes the fan to spin. When operating, the fan brings cool room air over the upper aluminum heat sink, thereby keeping the top side near room temperature while the lower side reaches the stove's temperature.

This fan will operate if the lower plate is heated to about 120° Fahrenheit. To test it, place a dark garden hose (full of water) outside on a sunny day.

Once it has heated, remove some of the water from the hose and place it into a plastic container. Put the fan in the container, touching the hot water, and it should spin.

This experiment suggests that water could be heated by the sun and stored in an insulated tank. Then at night the hot water could be used to generate electricity by using a Peltier cell generator. The commercial Peltier fan unit uses two cells and those cells make good contact (probably using thermal compound such as thermal grease, www.jameco.com, Part # 259151) with the hot and cold blocks of aluminum.

Wires from the Peltier cell go to the fan motor. These wires could be attached to a rechargeable battery, light, or other electrical load.

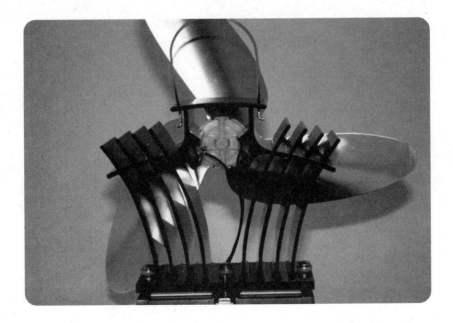

Remember, this Peltier cell requires a heat difference between the lower and upper aluminum heat transfer blocks. If the upper block gets too warm, electricity will no longer be generated.

18

WAVE GENERATOR

This is a simple device that captures energy from waves. Waves are (mostly) created by the wind, so this is indirectly a method of capturing wind energy. By using two yardsticks and a gear-driven motor (the motor operates as a generator), the bobbing up and down motion of waves can be used to generate electricity.

You could use this method to capture energy from the tides, but the motion of the tides (usually a foot or two up and down once or twice a day) is too small for effective "up and down" generation. Tremendous potential energy is available in tidal movement, but you need very large quantities of water (such as a bay) funneled through a narrow inlet to create the rush of water that could move a turbine.

MATERIALS AND TOOLS

2 yardsticks
Handsaw
Drill
Epoxy glue
2 4-40 screws, $3/8$ inch
Motor/generator (www.jameco.com, Part # 164785)
Wood block, 2 × 1 × ½ inches
4 1-amp diodes (www.radioshack.com, Part # 276-1102) (optional)

Built It

Cut one yardstick into two 18 inch pieces. Drill a ⅛ inch diameter hole 1 inch from the end of each stick. Mount the motor/generator to the yardsticks with two ⅜ inch long 4-40 screws.

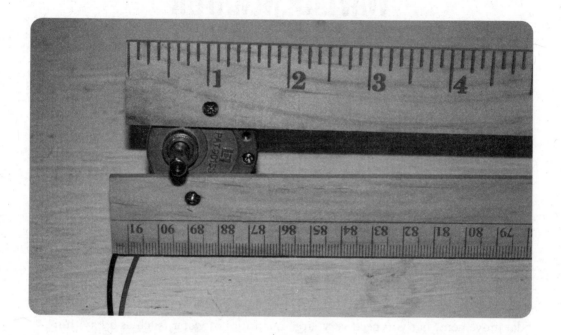

Take the second yardstick and drill a ⁷⁄₃₂ inch diameter hole 12 inches from one end.

Place epoxy glue into the hole, then press the motor shaft into it.

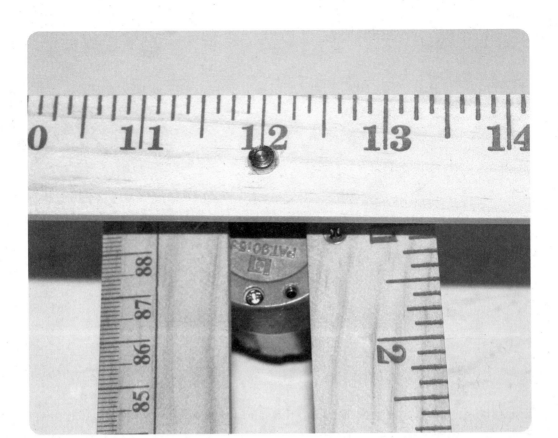

Glue a block of wood onto the end of the yardstick farthest from the motor shaft hole. This block will help the stick float. A foam ball or any other floating material could also be attached to the end of the stick.

The complete Wave Generator is now ready to operate.

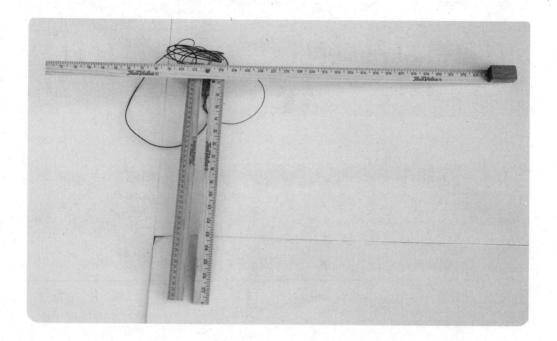

Insert the generator's 18 inch legs into the sand (or lake bottom) and watch the lever move up and down.

Because the lever moves up and down, the generator rotates one direction, then another. This results in positive voltage from the generator first appearing on one wire then on the other. To make this voltage more usable, you can run it through a diode bridge as shown here.

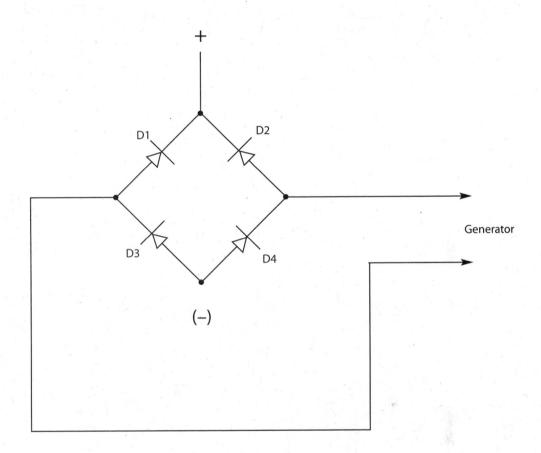

More to Think About

- Will a large block of foam make a better float than a block of wood?
- What happens to the motor/generator if a wave is too high?
- How would you make a Wave Generator that is not anchored to the earth?
- Will corrosion be a problem for a generator working near water?

19

LIGHT EFFICIENCY

Although most of this book is focused on ideas that can be developed to provide energy, you should also explore ways to reduce your energy needs. Right now, it is easier and less costly to save 90 watts than to generate additional electricity.

MATERIALS AND TOOLS

Desk lamp
100-watt incandescent bulb
23-watt compact fluorescent bulb
13-watt LED bulb (www.earthled.com, Part # Evolux)
Wattmeter (www.amazon.com, P3 International P4400 Electricity Usage Monitor)
Infrared thermometer (www.amazon.com, Kintrex IRT0421)

Explore It

You can use a desk lamp, a wattmeter, and an infrared thermometer to compare the efficiency of three different types of light bulbs.

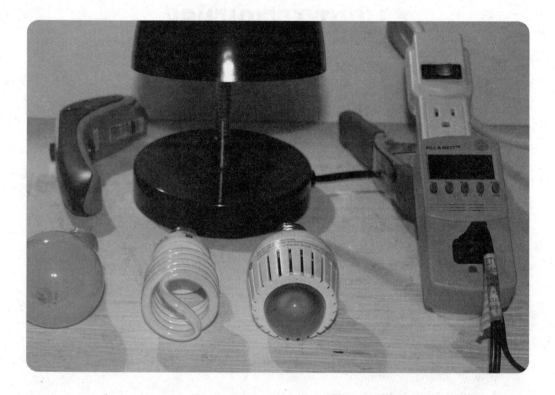

For the test, use a 100-watt incandescent bulb, a 23-watt compact fluorescent bulb, and a 13-watt LED bulb.

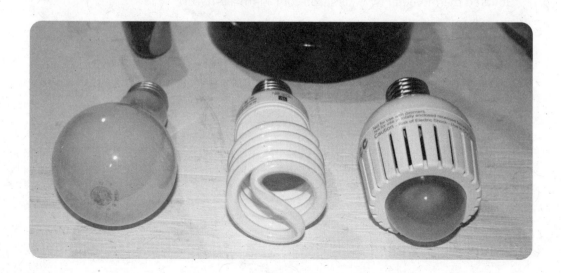

To find the temperature of a bulb, point the infrared thermometer at the bulbs until you find the hottest spot. To measure the wattage of a bulb, plug the wattmeter into the wall and plug the lamp with the bulb being tested into the wattmeter.

If your household voltage is normal, the incandescent bulb will use about 100 watts. The temperature of the bulb will be 160° Fahrenheit or more—too hot to touch. The 23-watt fluorescent will use about 23 watts. It will also reach a high temperature, too hot to touch. The 13-watt LED will consume 13 watts and barely get warm (maybe 90°F). You can touch the LED bulb while it is on without experiencing any pain.

Determining whether these three bulbs produce the same amount of light is difficult and is more of a subjective judgment than a scientific fact. The bulbs produce different "colors" of light. The human eye responds differently to varying wave-lengths (colors).

Light output can be measured—some bulbs list a "lumen" output. Light output is most useful when the "color" is useful to the human eye and is pleasing; blue/white colors are efficient, but considered cold and unpleasant.

The pattern of light emitted from the bulb also affects its usefulness for people. LED bulbs tend to throw their light in one direction while the other two bulbs cast light all around. In other words, the combination of bulb, fixture, and placement affects the light's suitability for humans.

The incandescent bulb is very wasteful, producing about 90 percent heat and 10 percent light. The fluorescent is better, producing about 50 percent heat and 50 percent light. The LED is best, producing about 10 percent heat and 90 percent light.

Today, LED bulbs are the most efficient, and the most expensive, bulbs available. Fluorescent bulbs are much more efficient than incandescents and are not too costly. However, fluorescent bulbs contain mercury and must be disposed of properly—this is not easy in most areas and it may lead to increased mercury pollution. A good neighborhood project would involve getting a merchant or school to serve as a collection point for old fluorescents and having someone periodically transport these to an approved disposal center.

More to Think About

- Count the lights in your house. How long are they on each day and how much power do they use?
- If you changed to efficient bulbs, how much energy could you save?
- How do people in your neighborhood dispose of fluorescent bulbs?

20

HUMAN-POWERED LIGHT

For far too many people, an untapped energy source is close and personal: body fat. Exercise is a good way to get rid of that fat (or just to stay healthy) and we might as well use that exercise for some good purpose, like lighting a room.

This project takes human activity (winding a hand-cranked generator) and stores the energy in a futuristic way (ultracapacitors) to power a very efficient LED light. The human-powered generator in this chapter is costly—perhaps your school can purchase one for the science lab.

MATERIALS AND TOOLS

Acrylic sheet, 12 × 12 inches, ½ inch thick (www.estreetplastics.com, Part # 1005001212)

Acrylic sheet, 12 × 12 inches, ¼ inch thick (www.estreetplastics.com, Part # 1002050100)

4 solid acrylic rods, 1½ inch diameter, 2 inches long (www.estreetplastics.com, Part # 5007524100)

Drill

6 medium screws

Screwdriver

On/off switch (www.jameco.com, Part # 22200)

Voltmeter (www.jameco.com, Part # 2095040)

Human-powered generator (www.windstreampower.com, Part # 454213)

Cable clamp

13 screws, $1/8$ inch diameter, $3/8$ inch long

12 ultracapacitors (www.tecategroup.com, Part # BCAP0350-E250)

Wire (#22 stranded)

Fuseholder (www.jameco.com, Part # 108792)

Acrylic tube, 1 inch outer diameter, 12 inches long (www.estreetplastics.com, Part # 6013012100)

Halogen desk lamp (www.walmart.com, Grandrich 20-Watt Halogen Desk Lamp)

Wire cutters

Pliers

2 wire connectors (www.jameco.com, Part # 302666)

Wire nut

LED light (http://store.earthled.com/products/earthled-directled-hl)

Build It

Start by attaching four 2 inch long (1½ inch diameter) rods to the 12 inch
square, ½ inch thick acrylic sheet. Predrill holes in the base and the rods, but first
practice using a piece of scrap wood. Find a hole size that will just allow a
medium-sized screw to slide in and out, then reduce that diameter by ¹⁄₁₆ inch. If
the predrilled holes are too small, the acrylic will crack when the screws are
added. Attach the base to the rods by inserting screws into the predrilled holes.

Drill holes in the **Upper Plate (19A)**, a 12 inch square, ¼ inch thick acrylic sheet, as shown on the template.

Insert the on/off switch and secure it with the mounting nut as shown.

Insert the voltmeter and secure it with its nut. *Do not overtighten*, as this can damage the meter.

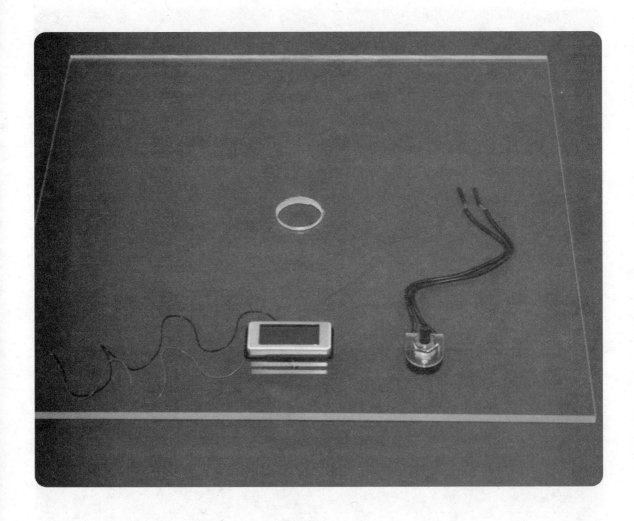

Drill a 7/64 inch hole in the lower base, ¼ inch from the edge and centered 6 inches from either end. Secure the generator cable to the base with a cable clamp fastened with a ⅜ inch long by ⅛ inch diameter metal screw.

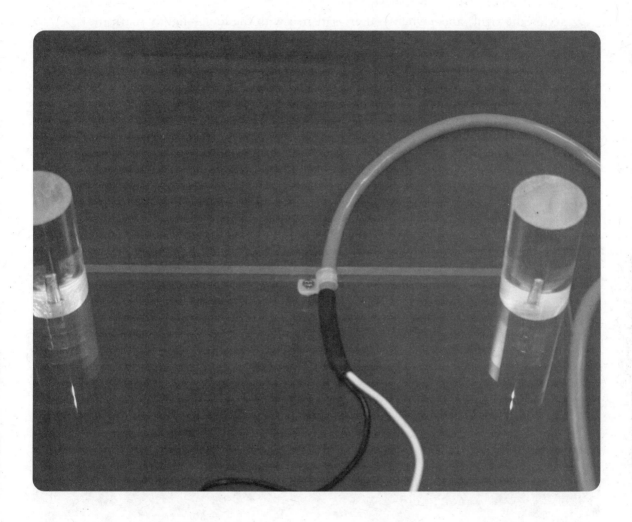

Using a screw (and a drilled pilot hole) fasten one of the ultracapacitors to the base, on the left side. The ultracapacitor has its own mounting bracket. Placement of the ultracapacitors is primarily a function of personal taste. I suggest placing the twelve ultracapacitors on the lower acrylic base (six on the left and six on the right) and—when you are satisfied with the look—lightly mark the proposed locations using a Sharpie pen.

Attach five more ultracapacitors to the base. Drill a $\frac{7}{64}$ inch hole in the lower base at each capacitor location. Using a $\frac{3}{8}$ inch long by $\frac{1}{8}$ inch diameter metal screw, insert the screw through the mounting tab on the ultracapacitor. As you mount each ultracapacitor, connect a wire from the top (positive) of each capacitor to the bottom (negative) of the next capacitor.

Fasten six more ultracapacitors to the right side of the base. Again, connect positive on each of these capacitors to negative on the next capacitor in the series.

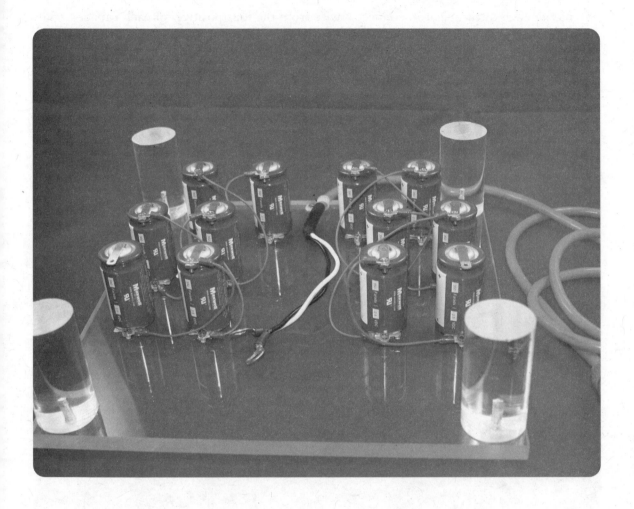

Attach the two final wires from the negative terminals (one on the left group, rear; one on the right group, rear) to the black wire from the generator cable. Fasten this combination to the lower base.

Attach a wire to the unused positive terminal on the left group and connect it to the unused positive terminal on the right group. Attach one end of a fuseholder to this terminal also. Attach the other end of the fuseholder to the positive wire (white) from the generator. Fasten this attachment point to the base with a screw.

Drill a ⅜ inch diameter hole in a 12 inch long piece of 1 inch acrylic tubing, ½ inch from the end.

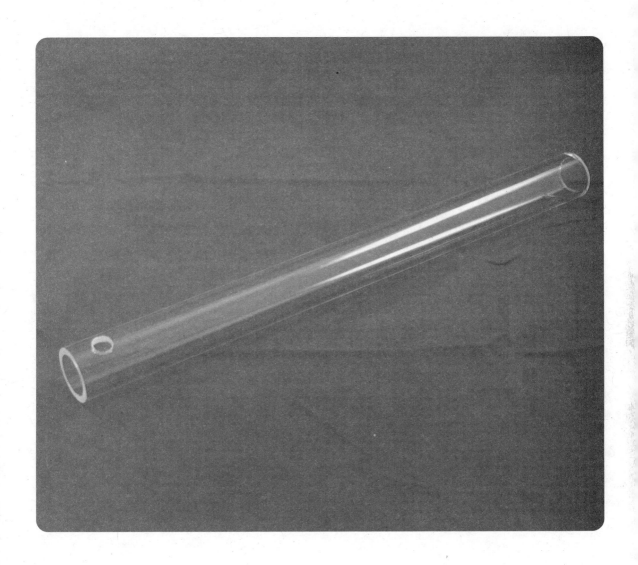

Obtain a halogen desk lamp and locate the screws that secure the protective glass shield.

Remove these screws.

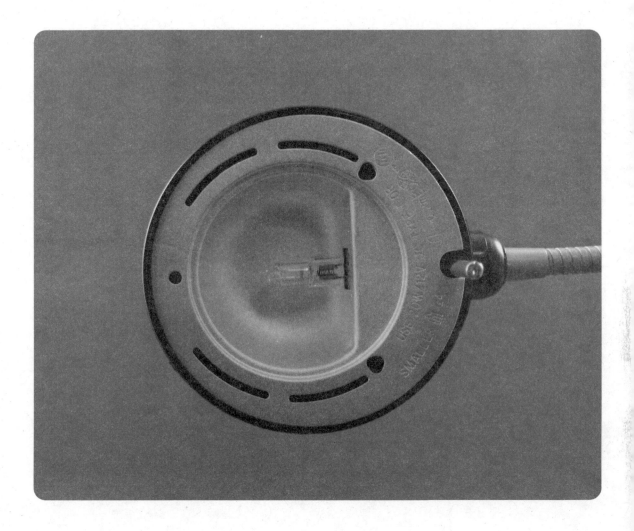

Remove the halogen lamp.

Return the screws to their holes. These screws hold the reflector in place.

Remove the bottom base cover from the desk lamp.

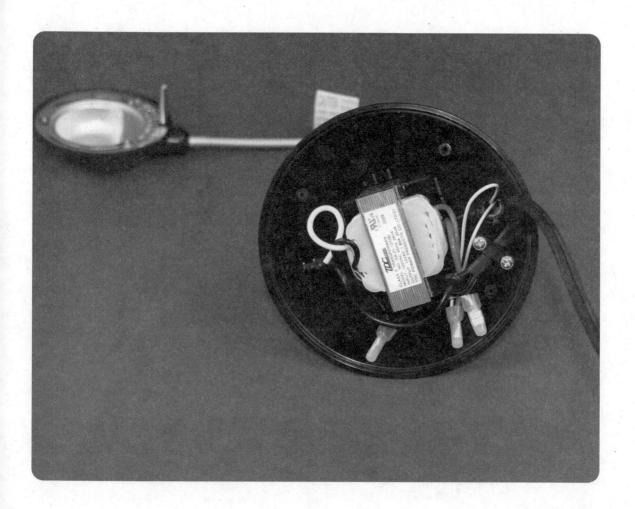

Cut wires and remove parts, leaving as much of the white wire (coming from the lamp head) as possible.

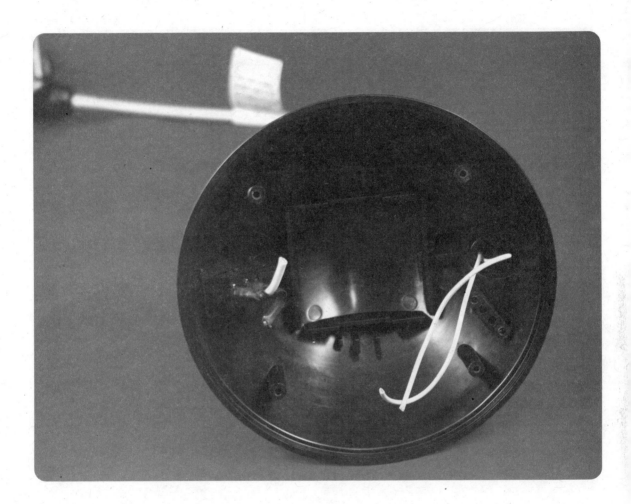

Grip the lamp neck with a set of pliers and twist the metal neck until it separates from the plastic base.

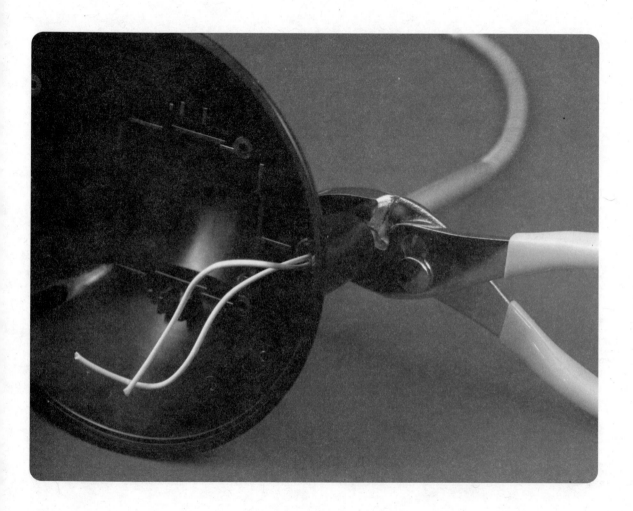

Carefully drill a ⅛ inch hole in each side of the lamp's neck—do not damage the insulation on the wires.

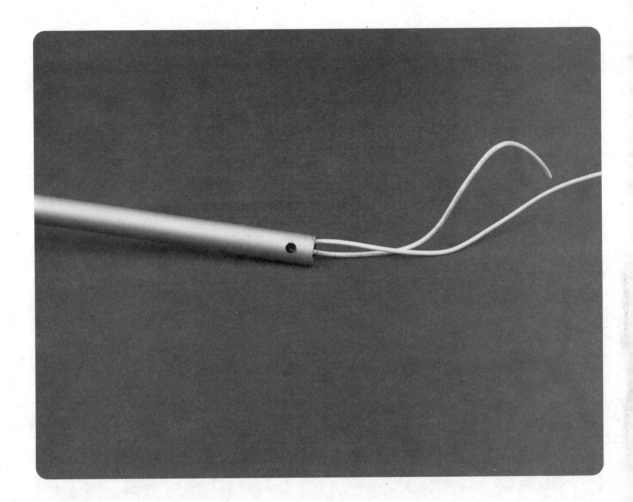

Pull the wires through the side holes. This is done so that the tubing will fit flush against the base and not crush the wires.

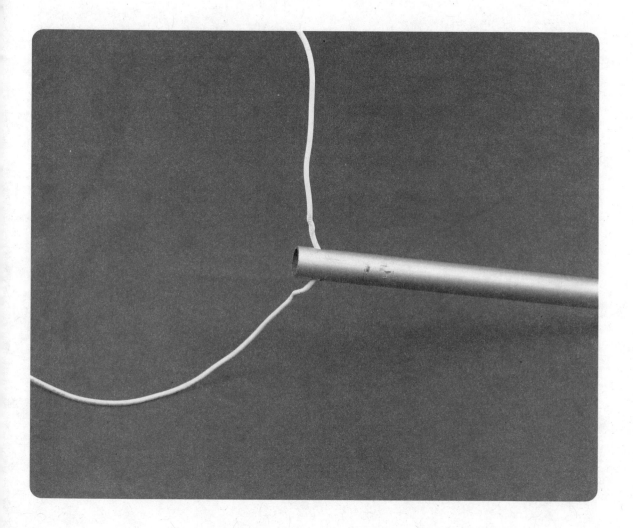

Insert the lamp's neck into the acrylic tube. The wires should be near the side.

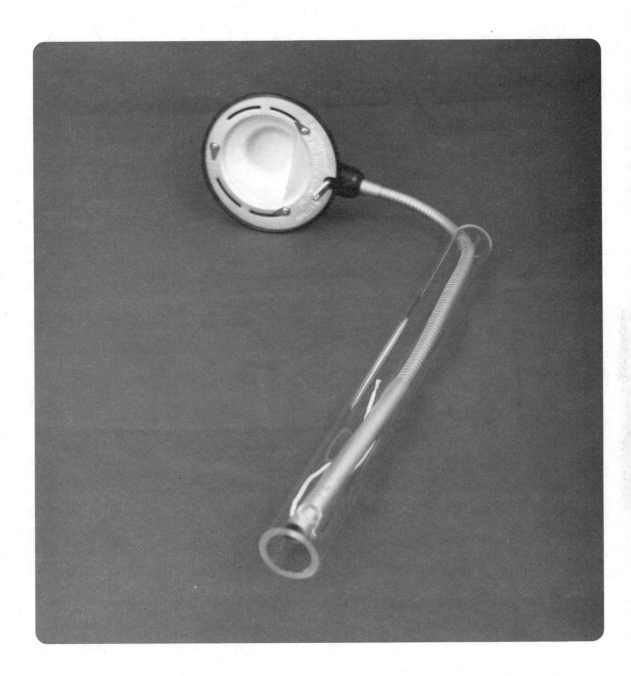

Insert the acrylic tube assembly through the large hole in the upper acrylic plate.

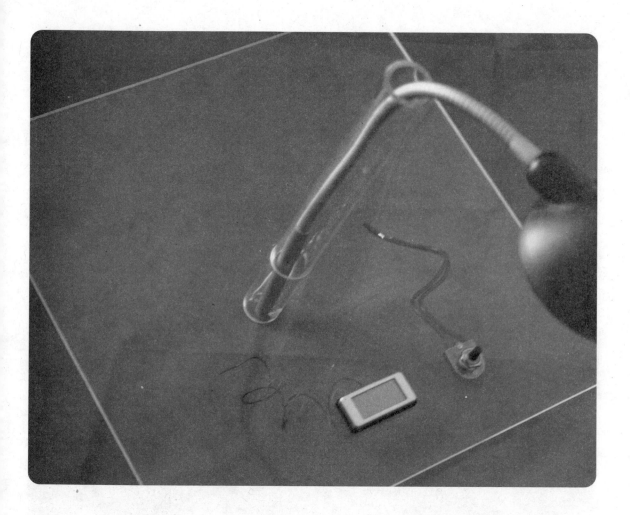

Pull the wires from the lamp's neck through the side hole in the acrylic tube.

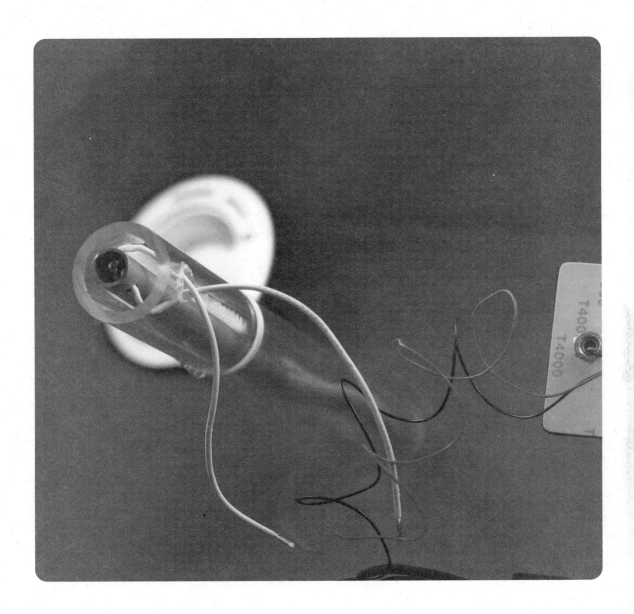

Take one wire from the lamp and crimp it into a connector with the black voltmeter lead. Attach this connector to the negative generator wire (left terminal on the base).

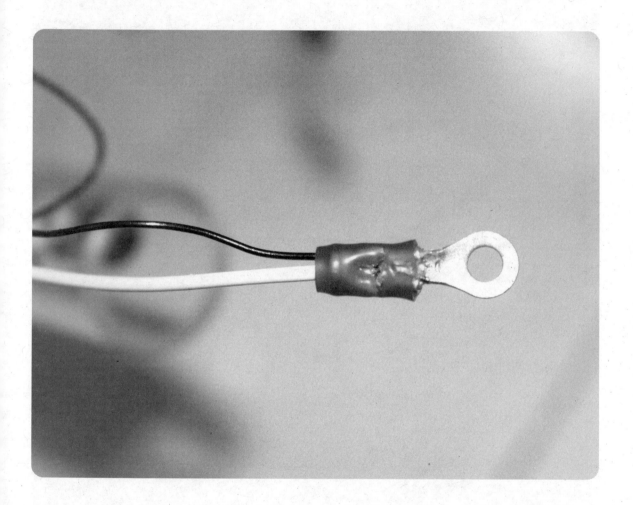

Take one wire from the on/off switch and crimp it into a connector with the red lead from the voltmeter. Attach this connector to the positive generator wire (right terminal on the base).

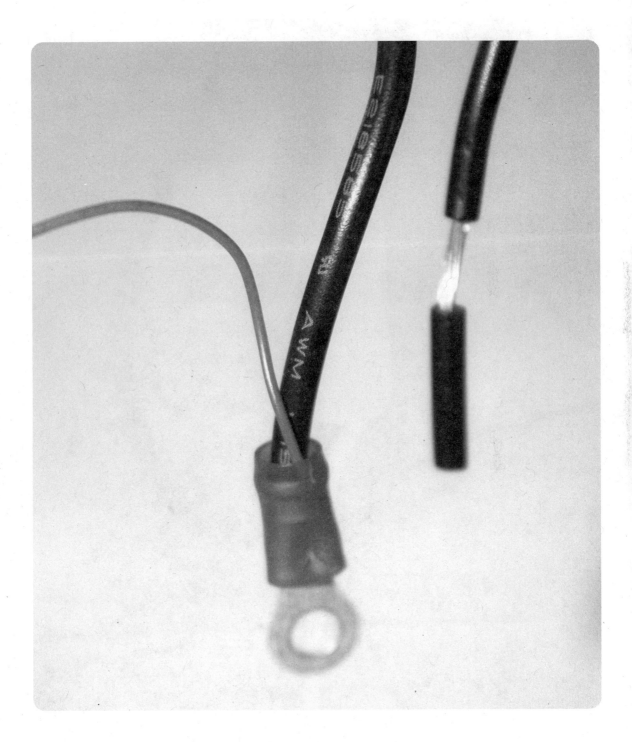

Take the other wire from the switch and connect it to the remaining lamp wire using a wire nut.

Insert the LED lamp into the lamp's head. The LED light pins are compatible with the halogen lamp pins.

Connect the generator cable to the generator.

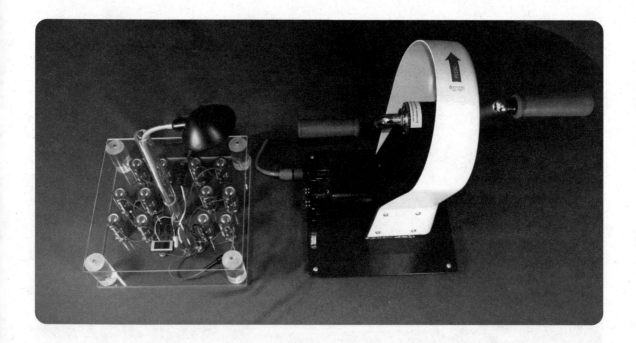

Crank the generator until you have 14 volts, as shown on your voltmeter. *Do not exceed 14.5 volts.* The ultracapacitors are rated for 15 volts, but they are the most costly component in this project, so it's best not to push the limit. Turn the switch on and you should have light. The light will stay on until you reach about 9 volts, about one hour.

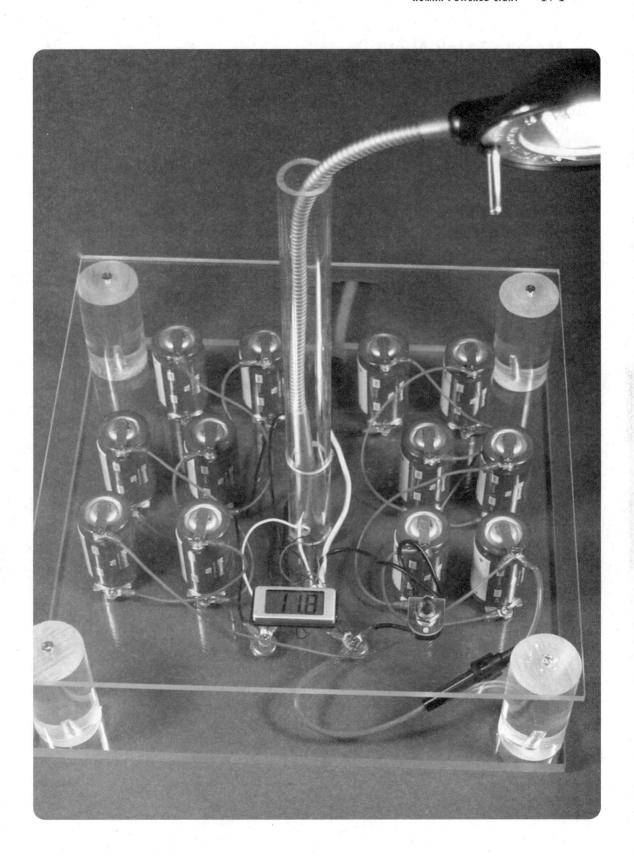

More to Think About

- Is it practical to use a human-powered generator to run an air conditioner?
- How could you use a human-powered generator to limit someone's TV time?
- How much power can an average human produce?
- How long would you be willing to wind a crank or sit on a bicycle and pedal?

This template is not to scale. Redraw using the measurements shown or photocopy at 200%.

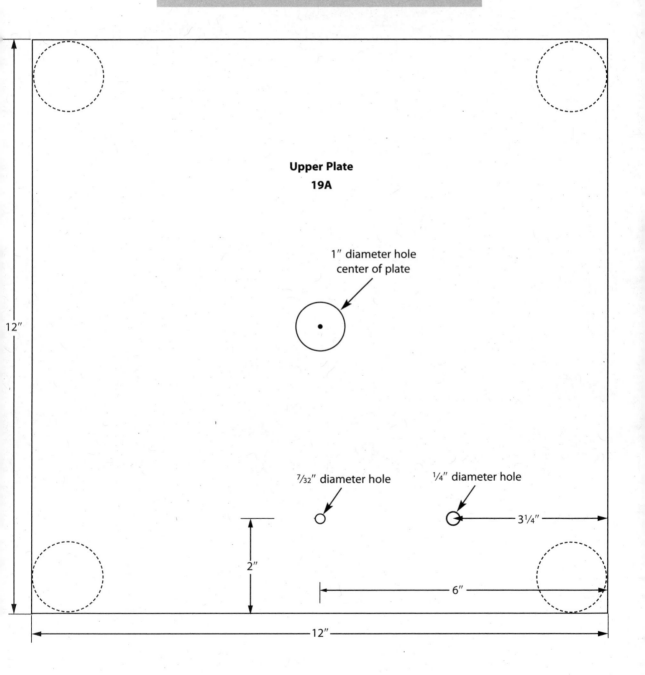

Upper Plate
19A

1″ diameter hole
center of plate

12″

$^{7}/_{32}$″ diameter hole

¼″ diameter hole

3¼″

2″

6″

12″

21

DIFFERENT DUNKING BIRD

In this chapter you will build a different type of dunking bird than you did in chapter 3. Its operation is very slow and takes eight hours or more for a complete up/down cycle. The motion is created by water going downhill, causing the pivot to unbalance, and water evaporating, causing the pivot to return to its original position.

MATERIALS AND TOOLS

Stainless steel sheet, ¼ × 3½ inches
Steel wire (#24), 3¼ inches long (or a small, straightened paper clip)
Epoxy glue
Soft facial tissue
Scissors
Fishing line
Paper clip
2 spray paint can lids, or other 2 inch tall platforms
Nuts or washers
Acrylic tube, 1 inch outer diameter, 1½ inches long (www.estreetplastics.com, Part # 6013012100)
Drill
Acrylic butter dish (http://homeandwine.com, Part # HWUA-4461-1a)
Water

Build It

Take a ¼ inch by 3½ inch piece of stainless steel and bend it 1½ inches from one end.

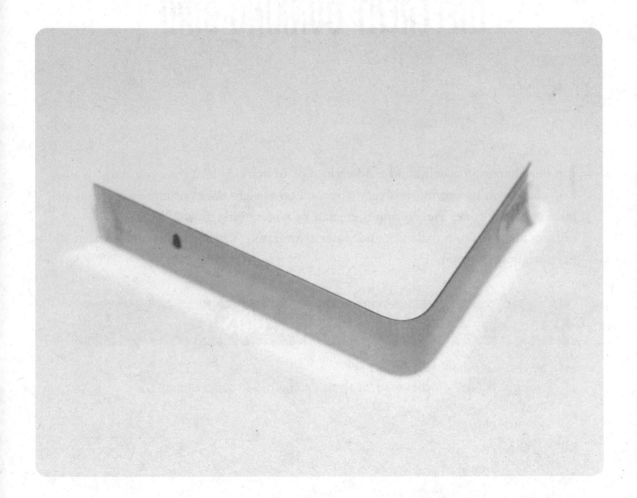

Glue the middle of a 3¼ inch piece of #24 steel wire to the back of the steel strip, ½ inch from the end of the longer side.

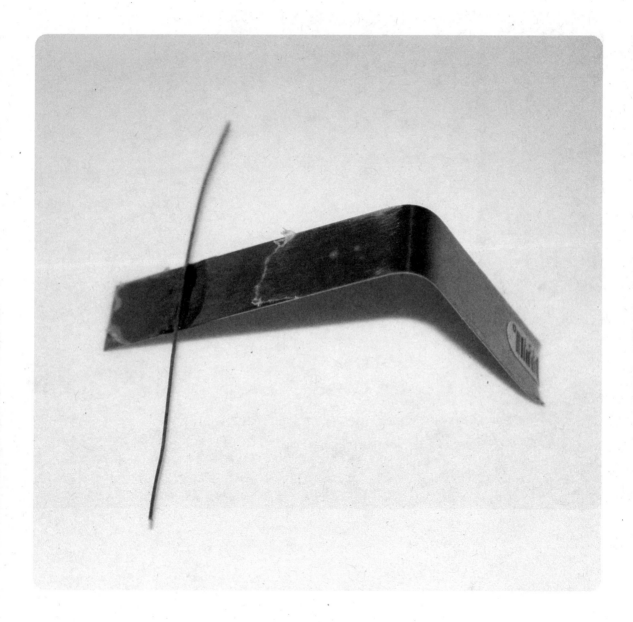

Find a square of soft facial tissue, the kind you use to blow your nose.

Fold the tissue into a triangular shape.

Cut the tissue into a triangle 2 inches from the point.

Place the tissue on the steel assembly with the metal bending up, as shown.

Poke tiny holes in the tissue and tie the tissue to the steel strip using fishing line.

Slide a paper clip, with one end bent up, onto the pointed end of the steel-and-tissue assembly, over the tissue.

Place the wire ends of the assembly on spray paint can lids, or cans, or wood blocks—anything about 2 inches tall.

Add weights, nuts, or washers to the upturned paper clip until the assembly is perfectly balanced.

Cut a 1½ inch piece of 1 inch diameter acrylic tubing.

Drill two ³⁄₁₆ inch diameter holes 2½ inches from the end and ⅜ inch from the top of an upside-down acrylic butter dish.

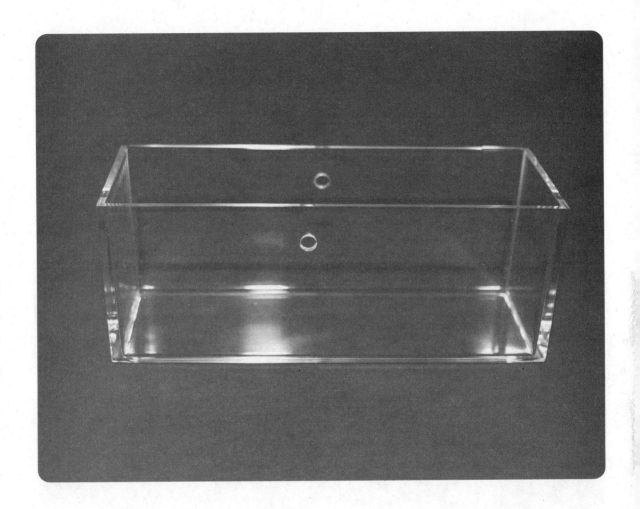

Glue the acrylic tubing upright 1½ inches from the end of the butter dish. Insert the wire ends of the tissue assembly into the holes. The bend in the stainless steel should be pointing down, into the butter dish.

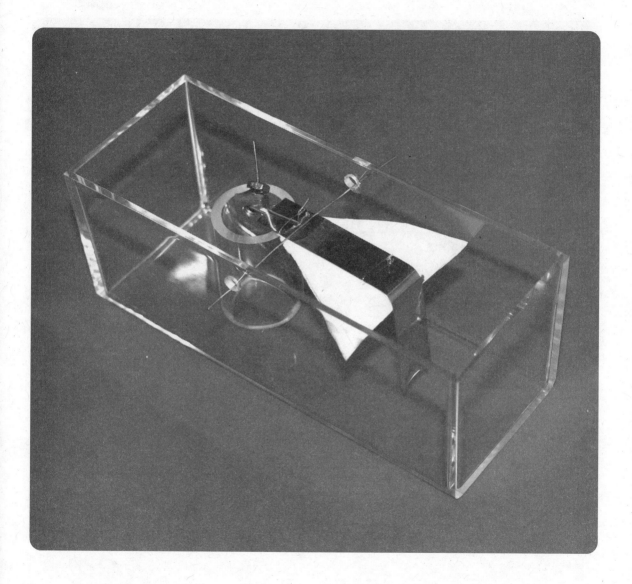

Lift up on the tissue assembly and fill the acrylic tube with water. Fill the tube as close to the top as possible. Release the tissue assembly. Water will flow up and out through the tissue (this is called capillary attraction). When enough water moves to the right of the wire, the assembly will become unbalanced and tip down to the right. This motion is caused by water moving from a higher level to a lower level.

After a few hours (depending on the humidity), the tissue will dry and the assembly will move back to the balanced position and start the cycle again.

More to Think About

- Does lower humidity speed the cycle?
- Will paper or a sponge work better than tissue paper?
- Does heat (sunlight) speed the cycle?
- What happens to the water in the tube?

22

ELECTRICITY IN THE GROUND

I f you want to experience the challenge of discovery, look to the earth beneath your feet. Believe it or not, electricity flows through the ground everywhere. This current is DC (direct current, not what the power company provides) and it is sometimes called telluric current.

MATERIALS AND TOOLS

2 metal rods, 12 inches long
Shovel or hammer
Voltmeter (www.jameco.com, Part # 117373)

Explore It

To examine this current you need to place rods in the ground. But before you drive any rods into your yard, even a few inches, think about underground utilities. The electrical, gas, phone, cable TV, and water companies all bury things near your home. Irrigation systems and other lines may also be buried in your yard. These companies do not always do a first-rate job at placing their lines underground. My cable TV and Internet connections travel through the "buried" cable shown here.

When you find an area that is free of utilities—try someplace away from homes and businesses—drive two metal rods about 8 inches into the ground. You can dig a hole and place dirt around the rods or drive them in with a hammer.

It is important to use rods of the same material. If you use different rods (like copper and aluminum), then your results may be somewhat skewed. Using rods of different materials results in an "earth battery," and some of the voltage you see will be due to a chemical reaction on the rods. Earth batteries were used in early telegraph systems, but their production of energy depends on the decomposition of the rods.

When you measure the voltage between the two rods with a voltmeter, you should record a low value, 100 millivolts to several hundred millivolts, and this value may change throughout the day. It can even shift from positive to negative.

ELECTRICITY IN THE GROUND** 195

Take notes and be scientific in your examination of this current. Keep track of the time of day, voltage, rod depth, and rod placement. Write down whether your rods are oriented in a north–south or east–west formation. Record the weather values, including temperature and rain.

Don't be surprised if the results seem random—just record and look for patterns. I had a set of rods connected to a voltmeter and the voltmeter was connected to a computer. When I examined the results one morning, I noticed that the voltage jumped from 400 millivolts to 4 volts—then went to about zero. When I checked the setup, I discovered that a wire jumper had been knocked loose from a rod. Based on the marks around the rod, I concluded that an armadillo had knocked the wire loose . . . and somehow created a 4-volt spike.

Be open to the possibilities. You may discover a new, usable source of energy. You may discover something about the Earth's crust or possibly a new way to detect animal movement.

More to Think About

- Do the results vary consistently from night to day?
- If you record results for a month, do you see any connection to the position of the moon?
- Which has more impact, depth of the rods or distance apart?
- If you bury metal plates instead of driving rods, do the results change?